CONVERSATIONS WITH THE CONROYS

The Conroy family at the SCETV-Radio studios in Columbia following their February 28, 2014, interview with Walter Edgar: Jim Conroy, Tim Conroy, Kathy Harvey, Pat Conroy, and Mike Conroy. Photograph by Fran Johnson, courtesy of SCETV

Conversations with
the CONROYS

Interviews with Pat Conroy and His Family

EDITED WITH AN

INTRODUCTION BY Walter Edgar

AFTERWORD BY Nikky Finney

The University of South Carolina Press

Published in Cooperation with South Carolina
Educational Television and the Humanities Council[SC]

© 2015 University of South Carolina

Published by the University of South Carolina Press
Columbia, South Carolina 29208

www.sc.edu/uscpress

Manufactured in the United States of America

24 23 22 21 20 19 18 17 16 15
10 9 8 7 6 5 4 3 2 1

Library of Congress Cataloging-in-Publication Data
can be found at http://catalog.loc.gov/.

ISBN: 978-1-61117-630-8 (cloth)
ISBN: 978-1-61117-631-5 (paperback)
ISBN: 978-1-61117-632-2 (ebook)

CONTENTS

Introduction

HOME AT LAST

The human mind is a fearful instrument of adaptation, and in nothing is this more clearly shown than in its mysterious powers of resilience, self-protection, and self-healing. Unless an event completely shatters the order of one's life, the mind, if it has youth and health and time enough, accepts the inevitable and gets itself ready for the next happening like a grimly dutiful American tourist who, or arriving at a new town, looks around him, takes his bearings, and says, "Well, where do I go from here?"

Thomas Wolfe, *You Can't Go Home Again*

For more than forty years I have plied my trade as historian in general—and historian of South Carolina specifically. While some in my profession have spurned local history as too provincial for their self-proclaimed cosmopolitanism, there are those of us who understand what John Adams meant when he said that to understand the American Revolution and American history, one needed to look first at local institutions. And, although the second president did not specifically say so, he implied that local history in context could help explain a larger story. That is the manner in which I approached writing this introduction to this collection of interviews with Pat Conroy and four of his siblings.

Each of these interviews needs to be looked at separately—and then with all the others as a whole. For each one in sequence reveals a bit more about Pat Conroy, his siblings, and their relationships to their parents, Frances "Peggy" Peek and Col. Donald Conroy, aka "the Great Santini." The conversations also let us follow the collective Conroy journeys of discovery to some place that they could at last consider home.

I first met Pat Conroy not in person, but through the observation of others. The first time I ever set eyes on Pat was in 1965, when my Davidson Wildcats were in Charleston to play the Citadel. The Wildcats were fantastic that year and trounced the Bulldogs 100–81. After the game, I saw one of the Citadel guards run over and speak to Davidson's All-American Fred Hetzel: just a few words and then a handshake. Fast forward a decade or so. Gene Brooker, one of my friends and a classmate of Pat's, was stricken with Guillain-Barré syndrome. Gene was hospitalized for months, and during that time Pat visited on numerous occasions to sit by his bedside for hours on end. At this point in his life, Pat Conroy had already hit the big time. This would have been a PR flack's dream: "Noted writer flies to the bedside of stricken classmate" with appropriate saccharine photographs. It didn't happen. I learned about these visits not from Pat, but from Gene's sister-in-law from Mobile. She and I had grown up together, and if there ever were a cynic, Prather Pipes Brooker was one. She called me to tell me about what Pat had been doing for Gene. In part because she said some in the media were beating up on Pat for being brash and insensitive about the feelings of others. And she wanted me to "set the record straight" in South Carolina about what a truly gentle man Pat Conroy was.

Over the years that followed, Pat's and my paths crossed at various meetings, but it was not until about twenty-five years ago that I had the pleasure of getting to know and appreciate the gentle man my friend had described. Since then, we have had numerous public and private conversations. Pat's brother Tim arranged one of the public conversations—a benefit for the South Carolina Autism Society held at the South Carolina State Museum. Afterward Pat signed books for hours. And, as is his custom, he never just "autographs" a book. He has a conversation with every person in line. At our "One Book, One Columbia" conversation in front of a crowd of nearly two thousand, a transcript of which is included in this book, Pat signed books and spoke with fans until 1:00 the next morning. This was Pat the extrovert and Pat the gentle man having a personal word with everyone who placed a book in front of him because he never forgets that readers and not critics make the lasting careers of writers. A Pat Conroy signing is always a master class in reader appreciation, and any young writer with ambitions for her or his future should pay close attention to how Conroy treats his audience.

Thus the context for my writing this introduction is based on my having read every book Pat Conroy has written, attended more public readings and presentations than I can remember, and on getting to know the private man. I had known the Conroy siblings other than Tim only through Pat.

In the conversations transcribed in this book, I hope that the reader will see and appreciate the private Pat Conroy. Most folks know the larger-than-life public Pat, always generous with his time and his words, but the private Pat is someone every bit as special.

Since 2000 I have participated in hundreds of radio interviews and conversations. It is not easy to translate the emotion and body language that accompany a person's comments. For that reason I generally insist that guests on my program come to the SCETV-Radio studio, so that I can read their faces and their body language and not just listen to their words. Tone of voice can mask feelings, but clenched fists, crossed arms, rolling eyes, grins, grimaces, and tears cannot.

When USC Press director Jonathan Haupt and I broached the subject of a Conroy family interview with Pat, he wasn't sure that Tim, Kathy, Mike, or Jim would participate. And, if all of them showed up, he was unsure of what would occur. After all, it would be the first time that the five siblings were willing to share with a nonfamily member their reactions to growing up with the Great Santini. While there was banter and joshing, there was a palpable tension in the studio on

February 28, 2014. This was not a conversation that was easy for any of them. But in that studio, it was the gentle Pat who was there to support his family as equal parts kind, thoughtful older brother and sage tribal elder. That same Pat was on stage for the conversation held several months later at the South Carolina Book Festival in front of hundreds and again in a more intimate conversation with two of his brothers in Charleston following his induction into the Citadel Athletics Hall of Fame.

During the course of these conversations, it became apparent that not only Pat but all the Conroy siblings had spent a greater part of their lives seeking some sort of "home." Through the impact of Pat's writing on them and their parents, especially their father, and their discussions with each other over the years, they appear to have found that home—a physical and an emotional one.

There is no doubt that Thomas Wolfe had a remarkable impact on Conroy's writing—not only in his style but also in wrestling with the problem of "home." When Pat was fifteen, the family moved to Beaufort, South Carolina. It was, he recalled, their twenty-third move, and he told his mother "'Mom, I ain't movin' again.' . . . And she said, 'Son, why don't you make Beaufort your hometown?'" The teenage Pat resolved to do just that. As Pat often says, he "latched on to Beaufort like a barnacle." But it took decades for the Conroy family as a whole to realize that, even though they were a peripatetic military family, Beaufort, South Carolina, was their home. Over the years it came to symbolize home for all the Conroys even if it were literally and consistently home only for some of them.

Beaufort was the scene of the event that triggered Pat's writing *The Great Santini*. It was an evening that Kathy, Jim, Tim, and Mike remembered down to the last detail—even the movie they had been to see that evening. With the publication of *The Great Santini* in 1976, life in the Conroy household became public knowledge. Kathy spoke for them all when she said that they "had a lifetime of secrets, and all of a sudden when you're reading your life in a book, it's not so secret anymore." Chillingly all agreed that Pat had not exaggerated the physical and mental abuse with which they had grown up. "If you knew the truth," said Jim, "it was much worse than the book."

Sharing their experiences with the rest of the world was not easy. Nevertheless all admitted that they loved the book when they read it. It was their story, and their father's reaction to it helped in reconciling him to his children.

Growing up with the Great Santini was often painful, but the siblings always had each other. They developed a sense of black humor to deal with their dysfunctional family. Sister Carol did not participate in the reunion conversations, but she is often the subject of them. However, she still maintains a connection with her sister and brothers and appears for weddings and funerals. "She's a good southern girl," said Mike, "no matter what."

The Conroys might have wondered about whether or not Beaufort was "home," but when they gathered for brother Tom's funeral, they found out. Tim said the Conroys "were blessed to be from South Carolina, because nobody rallies behind a family like South Carolinians do in time of need." Food, flowers, and a crowded church were tangible signs of the community's acceptance: "'your neighbors'—that you really didn't know were your neighbors, all of a sudden they're on your doorstep. To help you through this."

In these conversations Pat Conroy, Kathy Conroy Harvey, Jim Conroy, Tim Conroy, and Mike Conroy reveal that over the years in dealing with their childhood, their parents, and each other, they have at last found a home. In the opening sentence to *The Prince of Tides*, Pat wrote: "My wound is geography, it is also my anchorage, my port of call. . . ." The same could be said for his siblings. That geography, that anchorage, that port of call is unquestionably Beaufort, South Carolina.

WALTER EDGAR

An Evening with Pat Conroy

This conversation took place on February 27, 2014, in Columbia's Township Auditorium before an audience of more than two thousand. It was the keynote event for the city's One Book, One Columbia program, which had selected Pat's *My Reading Life* as its book for 2014. The interview later aired on SCETV-Radio's *Walter Edgar's Journal*.

WALTER EDGAR: Pat, we've done this before and one of the first questions that people ask, and particularly for these young writers out here, what was the one thing you would recommend that they do if they want to aspire to be a writer?

PAT CONROY: Read. You know my mother—Mom—we're not sure she graduated from high school. We know she went to high school. My grandmother and grandfather went to third grade. But when I was growing up, my mother read to me and my oldest sister every night, and she got in our heads that we were gonna be southern writers with great emphasis on the word *southern*. Now my father was a Chicago Irish Yankee who did not read, and I did not know if he could read. And I don't even know if he read any of the books I ever wrote about him.

But, you know, I had this powerful force in this mother who, when I write today, I still hear her voice, and she had this southern—She was from the hills of Alabama and Georgia, and she would always say, "Now Pat, it'd make me so proud if you would be a writer." And of course then *The Great Santini* came out. And her pride diminished overnight. And my father went crazy, and members of my family went nuts. And I had a grandmother, my dad's mother and father, never spoke to me again. That was it. And I learned very early that writing had severe consequences. But my mother berated me, and what she said was wonderful. She said, "In *The Great Santini* you made your father the strongest figure. I was by far the strongest person in that family. I was the one. Everything that happened in that family was 'cause of me. He was too dumb to come up against me. And you weren't a good enough writer to see it." And I said, "Mom, I saw it, but I needed you perfect for *The Great Santini*. I needed you to be the way I thought about you as a boy and that was perfect, and I had to have that." But I said, "Mom, I'll get to you later on down the line. And that's a promise."

WE: Well, you more or less did in *The Prince of Tides*, since she's there. She's a strong character. But if you had renamed *The Great Santini* for your mother, what would you have called it?

PC: *The Idiot Woman Who Married the Great Santini*. [*laughter*] You know, I could never figure that out growing up. I see this beautiful Mom with her southern, "How you?" and "How y'all?" And then we have this lump of solid protein, a blunt instrument, and that was Dad. It was funny to me when I'd see other kids and their fathers and, you know, their fathers hugging them and stuff like this, and for some reason I never got that. My brothers and sisters, we never got that. And then we moved every year being in the Marine Corps. So we grew up on federal property. So when I finally got to South Carolina I said, "Mom," it was my twenty-third move, and I was fifteen when I came here, and I said, "Mom, I ain't movin' again. You know, I don't care if I have to bury myself in Beaufort, I'm not moving." And she said, "Son, why don't you make Beaufort your hometown? You know we're gonna be here for two years at least, and this could be your hometown, and because Dad has served America, you can choose any place in the country. And they've gotta take you." So poor Beaufort, through no fault of their own, I latched like a barnacle onto that town, Walter. And through good and bad, whether they wanted it or not, and it is so much of an attachment that a guidebook came out ten years ago in which I'm listed as a native of Beaufort. And my neighbors on the Point could remember me riding my tricycle when I was a little boy. So fiction and nonfiction have certainly merged in these places.

WE: They accepted you, and you attached yourself to Beaufort because you talk about the influence Thomas Wolfe had on you, and you said you sort of kept tabs on introductory paragraphs and closing paragraphs of books. I sorta do the same thing, and one opening paragraph that I even cite in my history of South Carolina is, "My wound is geography, it is also my anchorage, my port of call; I grew up slowly beside the tides and marshes of Colleton," the opening prologue to *Prince of Tides*. You talk about Wolfe grabbing somebody with the opening lines of *Look Homeward Angel*. My friend, you grabbed at least South Carolinians because you may have been born elsewhere and moved twenty-three times, but I think there's pluff mud in your blood. [*applause*]

PC: You know, I stole that line from a Hallmark card. [*laughter*] No, I wrote that when I was in Rome, Italy. And I was missing South Carolina so badly. And I always, when I'm away from South Carolina, when I'm away from the low country, I'm always telling myself, why did I leave? What was I looking for? Why did I not just stay my whole life there? And it has been absolutely central to my whole writing life because I came to this place when I was a kid. I can't tell you how wonderful Beaufort was, Beaufort High School. I had this "king of the world" principal, Bill Dufford. I've got English teachers like Gene Norris and Millan Ellis. And I then go to the Citadel and there are five English majors in my class because being an English major at the Citadel in my time was an open admission I was gay. [*laughter*]

But I have had these teachers that loved me, and they encouraged me to write, and Gene Norris would come up, and he'd introduce me to people, introduce me to the poet laureate of South Carolina. He was the one that gave me Thomas Wolfe's *Look Homeward Angel*, and after that I went crazy for Wolfe. He took me the next summer up to see the house where Wolfe grew up in Asheville. He took me to the grave of Thomas Wolfe, and we were going to the house of Thomas Wolfe, and he'd say the things in the book, he'd say, "Right there, Pat, that's where the boarders used to sit after dinner, and Thomas Wolfe's mother would serve them dinner. And his sister would entertain them on the piano; that's the piano she used." And we went upstairs—there's a death scene in *Look Homeward Angel* that any time anybody dies in my novel, I'm always trying to write a better death scene than Thomas Wolfe did about his brother, Ben Wolfe, and it's one of the—I cracked up when I read it, I still cry when I read it today. And as Gene Norris, this great teacher, takes me through this house he said, "Now Pat, prepare yourself. There's the bed that Ben Wolfe died on. Thomas Wolfe's mother sat in that chair; his father sat in that chair; Thomas Wolfe sat in that chair in front of the bed; and they watched Ben drown to death on his own mucous." And so I'm looking at this stuff. So we're leaving the house. I'm profoundly moved, and as we're leaving, Walter, the North Carolina apples were coming in then, he jumps up, grabs me one, and says, "Eat it boy." So on the way back to Beaufort, I said, "Mr. Norris, why are you having me eat that apple?" And the great English teacher Gene Norris says, "Because it's high time for you to know there's a relationship between art and life." And that was my English teacher when I was fifteen years old.

WE: I think that particular story is interesting because, when you talk about reading, you use verbs that one would talk about eating; you talk about devouring words, devouring books, making them a part of you, and particularly words. And let's go back to Wolfe because clearly Thomas Wolfe had a tremendous impact on you. You even talk about it yourself. I think you said you could use five silver-tongued adjectives where one Anglo-Saxon word would suffice. And that sometimes is a complaint about Wolfe. But clearly you read this book Gene Norris gave to you. And I think the young people out there need to understand you don't just skim through a book; you read it, and then you reread it, and then you reread it again. And you still read it. But initially you read that book through three times, and that's not a short book.

PC: You know, when I tell people, young people about reading, and for me reading has done this: reading has changed my life utterly. It has changed everything about my life. Because I read, I wanted to write. Because I lived and read, I wanted to write stories, 'cause I lived in South Carolina, 'cause I went to the Citadel—and my Lord, the Citadel—I had stories flying out of me from everywhere. And because of this I wanted to write it down and have young kids read me the way I once read Thomas Wolfe. To me having a high school kid, a high school senior, picking up one of my books, reading it, there's no greater happiness. That to me is communication in a way that I dreamed about it when I was first putting a pen to paper. And I know about the life-changing quality of books. And I've read hundreds that, you know, I just, I'll read 'em, and I'll say, "My God, I wish I'd written that. I wish I could've written that." And then I'll say, "What can I steal from that book?" So I can then put it in one of my other books. Or what can I take from this that will make this particular thing ring in my own work?

So reading has been all-important to me. And the writing, you know, there's some that I do every year now. The only place in the world where *The Lords of Discipline* can be taught is a place in Arlington, Virginia. A high school. They come down to the Citadel every year, and I go up, and they've just read *The Lords of Discipline*, and I go up, and I talk to them about it, take them on a tour of campus. And it is heaven for me. It is absolutely unbelievably heavenly. What about your roommates? Where are they now? What was true? What is not true? And my brothers, some of whom are sitting here tonight, ashamed of me, horrified after listening to these stories once more. But my brothers have told me that over the years they have met at least seventy-five former roommates that I've had at the Citadel. [*laughter*] And I've even met 'em. The last time it happened was about ten years ago. This young woman and her two young children came up to me and said, "Now we will know the truth at last. My husband claims he was your roommate at the Citadel." Okay, if you have two young children and you were my roommate at the Citadel, you're dealing with trophy wives. Okay, this is not physically possible for men and women my age. So I look at this poor young man fully twenty years younger than me, and he's being horrified. His children are looking, and he's been caught. He's turned around in shame, his back to me. So I stand up and I say, "Roomie!" So he turns around and he comes roaring over. We hug. It turns out he was in my wedding. [*laughter*] And we're hugging. And we went down to get drunk at the Ark every night, and I did not drink in college. But it is a strange way fiction deals, you know. It's a funny thing with people.

And I was terrified of this book *The Death of Santini* coming out because I'm dealing with my brothers and sisters, my mother and father, not hidden in fiction, but as I saw them. And my poor brothers and sisters, they have been basically very good and very kind about this. And you are interviewing several of us tomorrow.

WE: Yes, we will do that. This program will later be aired on *Walter Edgar's Journal* on ETV-Radio and probably the only time that all the Conroy siblings have been, except for Carol, gathered in one room to talk about Santini. The first and maybe the only time will be tomorrow morning. We'll also air that on *Walter Edgar's Journal*. So any special precautions I need to take?

PC: Yes, here's one special precaution: you will find me a lot smarter, nicer, much grander a personality, much smoother, and much more charming than you will any of my sorry brothers and sisters. [*laughter*] It has been a burden on me my entire life. [*laughter*]

WE: Yes, but, but Pat, when the Great Santini was on his deathbed, the only person he said that he loved was your brother-in-law, Bobby Joe.

PC: My father, my father. My poor sister Carol is a poet in New York, so when Dad died, like when Mom died, the Conroy kids wanted to do it right. We wanted to send them out right. We as a family had suffered. These people are nuts. We were all crazy. We've all been in insane asylums for most of our life, hanging by our feet like monkeys. But when the end came, we wanted to do it correctly, so we split times up—and Dad was dying at my sister's house, my sister Kathy. Carol came down from New York, and I was relieving her one morning. And I drive up to the room where Dad is dying. I hear Carol screaming at my father, screaming, "Dad, Dad! You gotta tell me you love me, Dad! You gotta tell me you're proud of me, Dad. You just got to before you die. You got to do it." So I rush in, and she is screaming over him, "Tell me you love me. Tell me you love me, tell me you're proud of me!" So I grab Carol. I'm the oldest brother, and, you know, my brother Mike, he says birth order is the most important thing in family. And of course, because I'm number one, I loathed and hated all my younger siblings. But I go in to get Carol, and she's screaming at Dad. I said, "Carol, conference with the eldest." The tribal leader. [*laughter*]

So I get her out, and, Walter, she's crying, and she's upset. It's horrible. She's weeping, sobbing. And I said, "Carol, one thing I wanna tell you is Dad is dying, he's not going deaf. [*laughter*] And you don't have to scream at him. You know, he can hear you very well." And she is just beside herself, and she's going, "Pat, he's never told me he loved me in his whole life. He's never told me he's proud of me. I've made it as a poet in New York. It's so hard, it's so hard to make it as a poet. I've done it, and he's never told me he's proud of me at all. He's got to do it before he dies." And she's crying and weeping, and she says, "Has he ever told you he loves you or he's proud of you, Pat?" I said, "Well, now that you mention it, for the last thirty years my phone has rang at ten every morning, and it's Dad." And she says, "What does he say?" And I said, "Pat, have I ever told you how much I loved you? Have I ever told you how proud I am of you and the works you've done and the things you've accomplished? Have I ever just told you this, the whole thing, about my love is so extraordinary for you? My pride, I burst for pride for you." And I said, "Then he said, 'I only wish I felt the same way about Carol.'" So Carol is apoplectic. She's out of her mind. And I said, "Carol, I'm joking, all right?" [*laughter*] "Of course Dad has never said he loved me. Of course he's never said he's proud of me. I have no idea if he's read a word. I don't know if he knows I'm a writer. I don't know anything about it but that's not Bill Cosby dying in there, you know. That's the Great Santini. We have to translate how he loved us, and we can do that."

All right, so we go back in and I calm her down. Dad's gonna be dead in two days, by the way. I mean, he is, his voice is so weak by this time. So we go back in, Carol holds one hand, I hold the other and then my redneck brother-in-law, Bobby Joe Harvey, comes in early. And see, I don't have to explain to South Carolina what a redneck is. I was in North Dakota once and told this story—nothin', just nothin'. But Bobby Joe comes in, and he's doing something like rednecks do, like cleaning a wrench. He's just cleaning a wrench. [*laughter*] And he walks by us, and he says to me, "Hey college boy." I say, "Hey Bobby Joe, how you doin'?" "Hey college girl." "Hey Bobby Joe," Carol says. He says to my father, "Hey old man. How you doin'?" And my father says—my whole history of the Conroy family could be summed up by my father saying, two days before he died—"I love you Bobby Joe." [*laughter*] "I'm proud of you Bobby Joe." [*laughter*] And I had to stop my sister going for his throat. [*laughter*] And I think if she had made it that would've been it. That would've been the death of Santini right there.

WE: But that's the way he was your whole life.

PC: I think the Conroys can't do anything without it being a production. A grandfather died, and it's up in the hills, and it's a snake-handling family in the serious South. And I'm watching 'em, and they have the open casket, and they're going by, and my Aunt Lillian says, "I can't let him go. I can't let Cicero go." And these women in white say, "You gotta let him go, Lilly. You just got to." "I can't let him go. I just can't let him go." Next thing I know she leaps in with him, and I see a little eighty-year-old-year leg going over. She's on top of him. [*laughter*] It started something where if you love Cicero, you went in with him. So by the time I got there Cicero looked like he'd been dead for about three years in this thing. But it is the way of the Conroys. It is always melodrama. It is too much of too much, and it is never what we hope it's gonna be.

WE: You talk a lot about your mother's family, but your father's family from Chicago, they could not have been more different from one another. You've got some really battling genes in your body. You've got Irish folks from Chicago, very old-fashioned Catholic, and then you've got the Peeks, your momma's family.

PC: Yes. It was a disastrous marriage. Mom hated Dad's people. Just hated 'em, thought they were crass, crude. They were nice enough to hate us because we were southern. And we would go to Chicago, and they'd go, "Hey Pa-ayt, how y'all doin'?" [*laughter*] "You and your little redneck children wan' us to cook you some grits or some Aunt Jemima pancakes?" [*laughter*] And my mother would take that for about a half hour, and she'd be back in the car, and we would be heading down to South Carolina or Georgia again. They just could never forget it or leave it, and I think they have been most critical of *The Death of Santini*.

WE: One of the characters that really comes out not until your last one, *The Death of Santini*, is your mother's mother.

PC: Yeah.

WE: I mean, talk about an incredible grandma. And I think you need to talk about your mother's mother.

PC: Yes. You'd asked me before about the couples, beautiful couples from Atlanta, that after they read *The Prince of Tides*, I had this guy come up with his wife. And you've seen this in South Carolina a million times. A couple of you are these people. You know, the guy was, like president of KA, the fraternity at Carolina. And he had his eyes, like you know, hair like palomino and he's got these Weimaraner eyes and he's got a name like Prioleau Chastain. [*laughter*]

And so he walks up to the table, and he's married to this perfectly beautiful woman who was president of Tri Delts. [*laughter*] And it looked like a fusion of the gods and goddesses. [*laughter*] So he's sitting there, and he's read *The Prince of Tides,* and he says, "Hey Conroy, I finished your book and you've gotta admit your family's nuts, aren't they?" I said, "Yes, I do. I admit that very carefully." And then something about the guy irritated me, and I said, "How's your family, pal?" And then it's suddenly, "My family is glorious. They came over on the Mayflower, and they were governors of South Carolina and Georgia and senators and people that...." And I said, "That's great. Okay, let's get by all that. How far ...?" Y'all can play this right now in South Carolina. "How far do I have to go until I get to the first crazy in your family?" [*laughter*] And you gotta be truthful in this. I helped him out, "Dad, mom, brother, sister, aunts, uncle...." Okay, anybody not getting the hints off a couple of those? [*laughter*]

So anyways, I'm saying this to Chastain Prioleau or Prioleau Chastain, and his wife finally breaks. This beautiful girl finally breaks, and she says, "His mother's NUTS!" [*laughter*] And this is what I found when I go around—and my poor mother, why I could never talk about Stanny, her mother, my grandmother. When Mom was still alive, she simply denied this. Stanny was born up in the mountains of Alabama, a third grader, she told me, when she got married at eleven. And I remember when I was a little boy she said, "I wasn't even a woman yet." [*laughter*] And I'm thinking, my God, and I had no idea what that meant. [*laughter*] But Stanny ended up getting married, we think, nine times. There've been guesses as much as twelve. And when I first got a divorce, I remember telling Stanny I was getting divorced. She says, "You know, I've never believed in divorce. I've always believed in the sanctity of marriage." [*laughter*] And I said, "Funny you would say that, Stanny. You believed in the sanctity at least ten times that I've counted." And she said, "Men just love me. They came to me like bees to a flower."

And so I always found this utterly fascinating. And so my sister Carol, she's a Winthrop grad, fairest flower of the Southland, and I have just gotten fired from Daufuskie Island, so there was all this. Dad's in Vietnam, and the next day we're getting a picture taken to send to Dad. So my brothers and sisters, it was the seventies, and if you look in *The Death of Santini*, look at the picture in there, you'll see what is wrong with the seventies as you see how my brothers are dressed. [*laughter*] And so we're all in there, but Carol, the night before we're gonna have the photograph, she comes in, my grandmother's there, Stanny. And Carol says, "I've got to make an announcement." And you know, I'm thinking, okay. Carol is the family poet and the family drama queen, and she says, "I'm announcing to the family that Chris and I are lesbian lovers." So this is 1971, kids, so you know the time frame. Okay, my little four- and three-year-old daughters are there, everybody in the family's there, my brothers and sisters are there. And then my mother drops on the floor screaming and crying and says, "I knew it. I knew it. I'll never be a grandmother now." [*laughter*] And I said, "Mom, stand up and introduce yourself to my two daughters." [*laughter*] And, "I always knew this." She said, "You know, this was your father's fault." And in the Conroy family, it has to escalate in this way. And my mother says, "I can never accept it." And Carol screaming, "You must accept it. I'm your daughter. This is the love of my life." And my little daughter's saying, "Dad, what is a lesbian?" [*laughter*] And Stanny is on the side. Stanny is over there, my grandmother that had been married ten times, she said, "She's no lesbian. I've been around the world ten times. I met lots of lesbians." And then Stanny says one thing, ladies and gentlemen, and this is where my confusion as a human being and my confusion as a writer will always reside. There was one thing said I don't get it. Stanny kept saying over and over again, "Carol, you've never even been to Beirut." [*laughter*] It took me two years to realize that Stanny thought Carol was declaring herself from Lebanon. [*laughter*]

But, but Stanny represents something, Walter, that you caught this. There is always one breakout figure from all of our families. Stanny was it in my lifetime. I had never seen or heard of anything like it. Even after she died, they were showing reels, pictures of her, and we're seeing her, and my Uncle Joe is doing soundtrack. It was early, he thought he was gonna go into film. And he says, "Here we are in Jacksonville, my hometown. Yes, we're at the beach. Here we call it Jacksonville Beach. That's my wife and that's my wife's mother, Stanny." And Stanny is sitting there, she must be seventy years old, holding hands with a man at twenty-eight years old. And Uncle Joe is saying, "They just got married last week. Yes, there is an age differential but they seem to be getting along very, very well." [*laughter*]

But this is all part—and to add this with South Carolina and the stories I've heard from y'all, I could have no richer life. I don't think it exists in American fiction. I just don't. [*laughter*]

WE: That's why I write history of this state. I don't have to make it up. [*laughter and applause*] Let's get back to your writing, and I think particularly to the influence of Gene Norris. In all your writing and all your comments and ever since I've known you, this man, this great teacher had such an impact on you. You fell in love with Thomas Wolfe, and then you began to write Gene Norris very flowery essays. And so then he gave you *The Sun Also Rises*.

PC: That's right. Gene was one of these magnificent teachers and if there are any English teachers or any teachers at all in this audience, I fell in love with teachers. And if there are any students at this thing, here's what I found out about teachers: you can fall in love with 'em in the classrooms you go through in high school. And I simply fell in love with my teachers, you know. I fell in love with Bill Dufford, who was my principal, because I wanted to be a man like that, and I wanted to walk downtown in Beaufort and have people look at me with the same respect they had for Bill Dufford. Gene Norris, I wanted to be a man that thought the way he did. I came here in 1961. Do you know who Gene Norris introduced me to in 1962? Martin Luther King. You ever met a white boy who met Martin Luther King in 1962? And it was at Penn Center. Gene Norris took me up to meet the poet laureate Archibald Rutledge. And he knows I wanna be a writer then, and he has me dress up in a coat and tie. And we had a basketball game in Myrtle Beach on the way back, he says, "Okay now, I'm introducing you to this poet, he's the poet laureate of South Carolina. He lives on a plantation. And I've told him, I've called, and he's going to take you around." This is a teacher. I'm sixteen years old. So this is his free time. This is Saturday.

He takes me to Hampton Plantation, and this elegant man answers the door. And I've always wanted to look this, you know. Conroy doesn't look elegant. Archibald Rutledge takes me, and he says, "I hear you wanna be a writer, young man." And I said, "Yes, sir. I really do." He takes me up to his writing desk, he shows me what he's working on, and it was a poem. He hands it to me, asks me to read it, and said, "Are there any words you would change?" So I'm thinkin'—and he said, "Really, read it carefully." So I said, "One word, maybe this word could be stronger." He said, "Thank you very much. I'll consider that." He walked me all over the plantation. And he said, "Notice the details. This is where the deer sharpen their antlers on cypress knees. And over here is where Francis Marion ran from the British and swam across to one of my relative's house to escape them during the Revolutionary War." And so I'm completely floored by this. He serves me tea. It's terrific. We say goodbye. And I get in the car, and I'm thrilled. You know, I'm meetin' a great writer, and I am thrilled. I've never met a writer in my life. And so Gene, as we're driving off, he said, "Okay, what did you learn from that visit?" I said, "I learned to notice all the details. I've learned to notice things that are around me in nature to make sure I get the details right. And I learned Francis Marion escaped from the British." And he said, "If that's all you learned, you didn't learn anything." I said, "What are you talking about, Mr. Norris? I just told you everything he said." He said, "No, no. You're not as smart as I thought you were. You're not as good a student as I thought you were. What you should have learned, if you ever become a writer yourself, you now know how to treat a sixteen-year-old kid in South Carolina who wants to be a writer. Like you." [*applause*] And I still remember. Gene used to have me call up kids all over South Carolina when they were doing papers on me. I said, "Gene, I don't wanna do it." "Well, I know a little sixteen-year-old boy; he sure would've loved it if a writer had called him." "What's the number, Gene?" [*laughter*]

But it was that kind of teaching and because of Gene I learned this. Gene and I were best friends our entire lives. I didn't know I'd become a teacher's best friend. But Gene was just like me, he needed friends. And here's how close we became: I was one of the executors of Gene Norris's will. And you can become that good of friends with somebody who taught you to love literature when you were a boy and came into their classroom. [*applause*]

WE: I'd like to share with folks a story about Pat Conroy that a lot of folks don't know 'cause I've known you for a long time. You were classmates of a very good friend of mine, Gene Brooker, who is no longer with us. And Gene was a Citadel cadet, classmate of Pat's, and as a very young man he was struck down with Guillain-Barré syndrome. He was over here in the hospital for eighteen months. Pat was making movies. Pat came to Columbia any number of times to sit by the bed of his friend and read. Now, if you're making Hollywood movies, this is a public relations bonanza: "Classmate rushes to the bedside of seriously ill friend." Never a word to the press, but on a regular basis this man came up here and sat by the bedside of his dear friend and read to him and then went back about his business. And I think that tells you what kind of man Pat Conroy is. [*applause*]

Well, Pat, tell us a story. That's what you say, that's the secret. I think your mother wanted you to be a southern writer. That, I would say, is still what sets southern writers off from everybody else. You have a story to tell. So is there anything left in there that you'd like to share with the audience tonight?

PC: To me basically, when I come down to it, it seems like family is a love story. It takes a long time getting told, or a long time getting understood. The biggest shock I've had on this book tour with *The Death of Santini* is men and women coming up to me and saying my mother was the Great Santini. I don't think I could've survived that. I don't think it is possible for me to survive that. If my mother had been that way, I don't know I'd have gotten that through that childhood.

But our family, we've been through a lot. My family's been in two movies now. I hope there's one that's gonna get made of *The Death of Santini* because I want the people that play my brothers and sisters to be from that show *The Walking Dead*. Have y'all seen that? [*laughter*] And you know, I'd like to see these zombielike creatures play my brothers, where I am played by a very handsome, elegant young man who makes sense of the world.

What I loved when my father died, and I did, I loved this. We went to church. We knew it was gonna be horrible. We knew in some ways it was gonna be awful. And there was tension always because my sister wanted to have a poem for Dad, and I wanted to read a eulogy. And Carol would always torture me this way, and she did it a couple of nights before the funeral. And the way she tortured me was this, "Pat, I'm going to write a poem. You'll write prose, and you and I both know that prose is far inferior to poetry. And I will read my poetry after you get finished with your crappy prose." [*laughter*] And I said, "That's fine, Carol."

So we all rushed down. And then Father Jim is a priest who's dad's brother, and we have a three-hundred-pound statue down who was dad's sister, his sister Marge. The next day Father Jim, the worst speaker in the history of organized religion—[*laughter*]. We desperately tried to get him not to deliver, but he comes up, and he comes out. And the program's printed out, we're all ready and I will read my eulogy, then she will read her poem. She writes me a note and says, "Pat, I will never allow these priests to tell me what to do. They are part of the patriarchy, and I'm against it. I am not gonna read my poem until the priests are all off the altar." Okay, now the ceremony gets started, the funeral has started. So I'm reading this, I've got a printed thing with where everything's supposed to go, including the priests leaving with the casket. And I'm thinking, I'm now the only person besides Carol in the church that knows this. So I leaned down and, I regret this, but I'm related to my father, and I went through the plebe system at the Citadel. So I leaned down and I'm completely unnerved, it's the only funeral of my father I've ever been to. [laughter] I don't know quite how to feel. So Carol's not gonna get up, she's gonna sit there, and the whole church is gonna be looking at me. Carol, give me a break! And I turned. Now, my brothers and sisters, who are in the audience, go down on one knee and begin shooting me the bird. And I contend this does not happen at most southern funerals. [laughter] And my back is turned, or there would've been a fist fight. So I later said, "How many birds were thrown?" And my brother Mike always low keys things, and he says, "I think there were only 50." [laughter] And my brother Tim always exaggerates things, he's like me. He says, "I'd say 150, 200." [laughter]

And I said, this rarely happens in an American funeral, but it was so typical of what happens when I write books. I never worry about going too much, doing too much. People tell me stories in South Carolina that I will sit and be staggered by simply the melodrama or the dramatics; a sister, a brother, somebody will be in there. You know, I come here tonight, there's a man in the back who scares everybody that comes here. He says, "You wanna a Coke?" And you lift up a thing where you get a Coke, and a rattlesnake springs out at your face. And he said, "I've scared Springsteen, I scared Seinfeld, I've scared everybody that's come through here." And I say, "You know, South Carolina is hard to top." [laughter] This guy's been scaring people with a rattlesnake for forty years in this thing, and I didn't know it till tonight. My gosh.

WE: Pat, it's time for us to wrap up. Any last words for our audience before we sign out today?

PC: One thing that I do think: reading is still the one place you can go to be alone in a very loud and noisy America.

WE: Pat Conroy. [*applause*]

PC: And it was wonderful to see y'all tonight. [*applause*] Thank y'all very much.

Peggy Conroy, Atlanta, Georgia, 1946

Don Conroy holding infant Pat Conroy, Virginia, May 1948

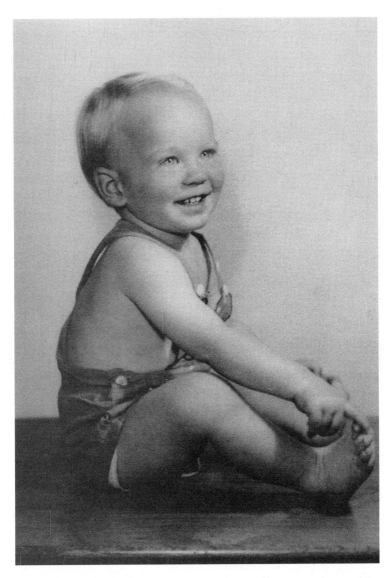

Pat Conroy at age two, Atlanta, 1947

Peggy and Pat Conroy, San Juan Capistrano, California, circa 1947

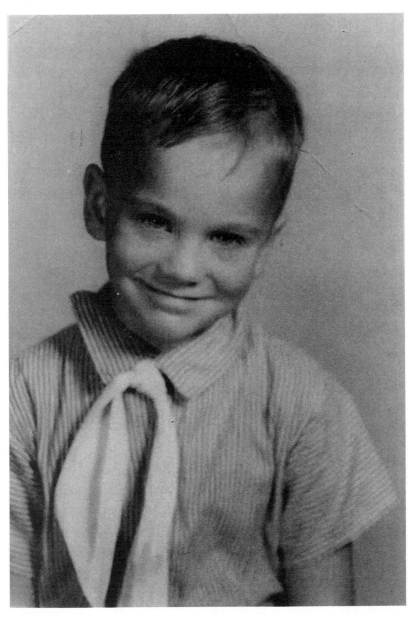

Pat Conroy, Cherry Point, North Carolina, 1950 or 1951

Carol and Pat Conroy, ages three and six, Cherry Point

Carol Conroy, Pat Conroy, Jasper Peek (maternal grandfather), Kathy Conroy, Peggy Conroy, Don Conroy, Tim Conroy, Jim Conroy, and Mike Conroy, Fairfax County, Virginia, October 1958

Jim (top), Tom (on Peggy's lap), Mike, Peggy, Kathy (back),
Pat, Tim, and Carol Conroy, Omaha, Nebraska, circa 1963

ABOVE: Carol, Kathy, Don, Jim (on Don's knee), Pat, Peggy, Tim (on Peggy's lap), and Mike Conroy, Maryland, circa 1958

Carol, Tim (top), Tom (bottom), and Pat Conroy, Omaha, circa 1963

Pat Conroy (number 22) playing for the Citadel Bulldogs basketball team, circa 1964

Pat Conroy in his Citadel cadet uniform

Col. Donald Conroy in his U.S. Marine Corps uniform,
Pensacola, Florida, circa 1967

Don and Peggy Conroy, Hawaii, circa 1971

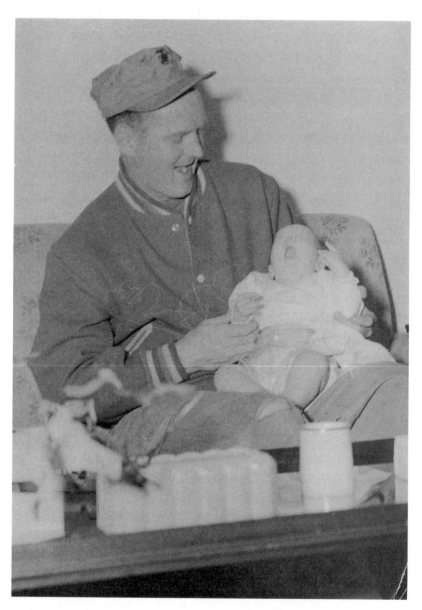

Don Conroy holding Mike, Cherry Point, North Carolina, 1952

Mike Conroy, age four,
Orlando, Florida

Mike Conroy, age sixteen,
Pensacola, Florida

Jim Conroy, age nine,
Omaha, Nebraska

Jim Conroy, age sixteen,
Pensacola, Florida

Kathy Conroy, age nine, Beaufort, South Carolina

Kathy Conroy, age nineteen, at the Sunshine '72 Festival Concert in Oahu, Hawaii

Tim Conroy, age six,
Omaha, Nebraska

Tim Conroy, age sixteen,
Beaufort, South Carolina

The Conroys in Pensacola, 1968: (seated) Peggy, Tim, Tom, and Don;
(standing) Jim, Carol, Pat, Kathy, and Mike

Tim and Jim Conroy with Kathy in her First Communion dress,
Spring Valley, Virginia, circa 1960

Stanny with Don and Tom
Conroy, Rock Springs,
Florida, circa 1965

Stanny in Atlanta,
circa 1950

Don Conroy's siblings Father James Patrick "Jim" Conroy
and Sister Margaret "Marge" Conroy in Minnesota

Don Conroy's parents with Sister Marge and Father Jim, Chicago, circa 1964

James Patrick Conroy Sr., Father Jim, Sister Marge,
and Don Conroy, Davenport, Iowa, 1985

Pat Conroy and Family

This first Conroy family reunion conversation was recorded in the studios of SCETV-Radio for *Walter Edgar's Journal* on February 28, 2014—the morning after Pat's public conversation in Columbia. Pat, his sister Kathy, and his brothers Mike, Jim, and Tim had their first-ever group discussion of their childhood experiences.

WALTER EDGAR: Welcome to *Walter Edgar's Journal*. Today my guests will be author Pat Conroy and four of his siblings, Kathy, Mike, Jim, and Tim. And we're gonna talk about what it was like growing up with the Great Santini. That novel had a tremendous impact on the Conroy clan, and as we'll find out during our conversation, brought them closer together. And so ladies and gentlemen, welcome to the *Journal*.

PAT CONROY: I'd like to apologize for everything my family is about to say and reveal about me in this next hour.

WE: Let's start off. Pat, I wanna ask your siblings if the world you depicted in *The Great Santini* was their world. And Tim, how would you react to that? You were a real youngster then.

TIM CONROY: I was five years old when Pat was eighteen. But, you know, the intensity of what he captured in *The Great Santini* was exactly what I recall and remember. I can't describe the dysfunction of those times. I think Pat caught it—and I really think that the movie caught the spirit of the family. Of course Jim has the best line about that movie, ever.

JIM CONROY: [*laughter*] I have no idea what line he's talking about.

PC: Yeah, I do. I know exactly the line.

JC: Do ya?

PC: Yes. You were at the opening in Beaufort, South Carolina, on the front row with the family.

And Robert Duvall beats up the entire family on screen. And of course all the people in Beaufort are looking horrified 'cause we're there. And Jim leans down the row of kids and says, "Bambi. Somebody should've taught Duvall to really know how to beat up a family. He looks like Bambi compared to Dad." And the kids fell apart on the front row.

KATHY HARVEY: I think the amazing thing about *The Great Santini* is that Pat was able to capture my dad as such a loveable character. And I know that might surprise a lot of you, but my dad was really tough but there was something so likeable about him in that book.

WE: We know that Pat suffered physically, but Kathy, what about you and Carol, the girls?

KH: My dad really didn't physically abuse me. My dad was more into the terror and fear.

WE: The verbal?

KH: Very much verbal.

WE: Yeah. Well, some of the way he acted, and I used this last night when we had an earlier conversation about the Great Santini being on his deathbed. Your older sister Carol just wanted him to say that he loved her and appreciated her. But the only person that he said he loved and appreciated was your husband, Bobby Joe, with Carol hearing that. I mean, is that an example of the experiences that you had?

KH: It was impossible for Don to say he loved us or was proud of us. It never happened.

WE: It never happened. But he did say that about your husband.

KH: He sure did.

WE: Pat?

PC: And I can't understand why he was not proud of me. I can certain understand why he was not proud of the younger children.

KH: [laughter]

WE: Jim, you're looking very stoic right now.

TC: Cause he's the dark one.

PC: The dark one, the dark one, yes. [laughter]

WE: Now, when you say the dark one, what does that mean?

JC: I have no idea, Walter.

WE: Okay, what does the, what does the—

PC: Tim, would you like to?

TC: Well Jim, he probably has the most remarkable memory of anybody in the family.

JC: It's not saying a lot, Walter, don't look at me like that. [laughter]

TC: And he can sometimes be light and funny and see things in incredible ways, but sometimes there're moments where Jim can see the truth of it all. And that truth sometimes is a dark truth, and it just comes out. He was such a happy kid, at times, and wanted—

PC: He was just a joyful, happy little boy, born to a monster.

JC: I think they're implying that I'm no longer a happy kid. [laughter]

PC: Jim has a son, Michael, just like him. And he's, you know, this kid, he's all over the place, he's funny. Dad would have killed him if Dad had been raising him. And we were once sitting around, and someone said, "Michael is just like Jim, his father, was when he was a little boy," and what did you say?

TC: Well I'm not exactly sure what you're referring to now, but Michael has the same bravado as Jim. I mean, Michael would say he was good and great at everything, and he may have not ever had tried it before, but it is just like Jim's great bravado when he was a kid.

PC: And then Tim once said Jim was bright, happy, vivacious until Dad broke his spirit. [laughter] And turned him into the dark one who sits before us today.

KH: But I think it was that humor that saved us.

WE: So where did y'all get the humor? From your mom?

TC: No!

JC: We all have different fathers. [*laughter*]

PC: Mom did not have much of a sense of humor. And I didn't know Dad had one until after Mom divorced him. I just didn't know he was funny 'cause he never tried to be funny when I was a kid, never made me laugh. I didn't laugh at him at all. Now you may have caught the late-blooming Dad where he was funny towards the end of his life.

KH: It wasn't funny. He really wasn't funny, I don't think, until *The Great Santini* came out. And to me when he read the book, after he got over his anger, I think he decided to be very competitive with Pat and show Pat that's not the way this is and that's not the person he was. But to me in the process he fell in love with his children.

WE: *The Great Santini*, the publication of that book and the movie, which I think all of you say that the movie, the impression that that gave, you were happy with that or you were comfortable with that?

KH: Loved it.

WE: You loved it.

TC: I enjoyed it. I thought it was very good, so I enjoyed it.

WE: Jim, who played you on screen?

JC: He kind of incorporated all the kids into a couple of characters, so, in fact there were four kids in *Great Santini* and he actually had six brothers and sisters. He's forgotten about some of us, but now he's, in that book he has—

PC: I'm getting back to you as I age. [*laughter*]

WE: So, let's just start, when the book comes out, and let's talk about your individual reactions to *The Great Santini*. Jim?

JC: The book came out and it was interesting 'cause we all got a copy that night, and I remember distinctly that Mike, Kathy, and I started reading the book at the same time, and we all finished the book that night at the same time. And it was funny because I ran into Kathy or Mike and at the end of the book, I'm sitting there with tears in my eyes. And I'm sitting there, and I'm looking at Kathy, and she's just at the same part, she's just finishing and, you know, at the end of *The Great Santini* my father dies. And I sit there, and we're together, and I look at her, and I go, "Kathy, we're crying and I'm glad he died." [*laughter*] It's a great ending; yet the book is sad at the ending, so we kinda chuckled over that.

WE: Actually that is a tribute to your older brother's writing.

JC: Oh absolutely. And we agree to that; we thought it was a great book.

WE: Yeah. Kathy?

KH: I think the book was so difficult to read because we'd had a lifetime of secrets, and all of a sudden when you're reading your life in a book it's not so secret anymore. So I think that was a really difficult thing for me.

WE: Tim?

TC: You know, when I read the book what was so hard about that book for me was the scene on the green in the Point in Beaufort when the Great Santini and the character Ben confronted each other. Because I knew where that scene came from, I lived that scene.

WE: One second, Tim—describe that scene for our listeners because they may not remember that.

TC: Well, the reality of the scene, I think the inspiration, was a night that my mother and father went to Parris Island for a movie. And we all went to see the movie, and my father went to the O Club and probably had a few drinks and came back. There was very bad tension between my mother and father that night, and there was a scene in the parking lot where my mom tried to drive off and my father hit my mother. Several times. And, you know, as a kid in the backseat of the car and having my mother say, "Lock the door. Lock the door." And having that whole thing unfold, and then come back into Pat's house with his family and his kids and have that terrible scene in the book take place where I knew what parts were real and what parts were not necessarily real. And the real scene was much worse to me than the book scene. And Pat, you may wanna comment on some of that.

PC: You know, it's one of those things, like a lot for me in our life. It was too emotional to take it all in for me. And what worried me about that night is that I'd never told my wife that I came from a family like this. I'd never told anybody I'd been belted around by Dad, been hit by Dad, been abused by Dad. I hadn't told a soul. So all of a sudden I wake up upstairs, and it's the first time I've ever owned a house. And I'm very proud 'cause, you know, none of us kids, we didn't live in a house we owned, so I owned a house before Mom and Dad. And so I'm upstairs sleeping when they get back from the movie and I hear the old sound. I hear the slaps goin' on, Mom crying, kids crying. And I tiptoed down 'cause I didn't wanna wake Barbara, my wife. And I tiptoed down and I see Dad swatting Mom, and I went crazy. And I just went absolutely nuts, drove Dad through the front door. And I was still physically terrified of Dad, but luckily for me he was drunk. And so we went out, and I was kicking Dad. I was even slapping him, and I put him in the car, and then he drove off, and he was weaving down the street so badly. And later I came in, and this is when it all came out. The kids are crying, and my whole thing with the kids was trying to keep them quiet so they did not irritate Dad. And so I was tryin' to calm 'em down, because this usually was safety, if I could get everybody quiet.

WE: These are your children or these are—

PC: No, these are my brothers and sisters. My children did not wake up during this.

JC: Pat's children woke up, and they were a little loud, and Pat hit 'em.

TC: The dark one speaks.

PC: See, this is the dark one that we have.

JC: I remember that night too, and running into your house and running up the stairs to get away from Dad.

WE: All right Jim, how old were you then?

JC: I was just finishing ninth grade.

WE: Okay.

JC: And we were moving to Beaufort, South Carolina, and my father was about to go to Vietnam. Which was a good thing. Anyway, I was tryin' to get upstairs, and I ran across Barbara at the top of the stairs. And Barbara said, "What's goin' on?" I said, "Barbara, I'm gonna give you some advice. It's a real good idea not to go downstairs right now." [*laughter*] And she said, "This is my house. I can go anywhere I want." And I said, "Barbara, you go right ahead, but it's a real good idea to stay upstairs." [*laughter*]

WE: And Tim, you were obviously much younger than that at this point.

TC: Yeah. I was in the sixth grade. You know, it was just a horrible night. I remember the drive back, uh, from Parris Island—

WE: And your mom was driving.

TC: My dad was driving. He had forced his way into the car, slapped my mom, slapped us. My head was pressed against the window, and I thought about opening the door and just rolling out. It was it was one of those scenes that shaped me.

WE: Do you remember the movie?

TC: *Butch Cassidy and the Sundance Kid.*

WE: Good. Very good. [*laughter*]

WE: And Kathy?

KH: I was a senior in high school. We had just moved to Beaufort, and I was gonna be starting my senior year there when this happened. And as horrible as the night was, there was something really wonderful about someone being more powerful than Don.

PC: And what was good for me, it was the beginning of *The Great Santini* for me. Because Barbara is at the top of the stairs, "What's going on in my house?" And I'm down there at the bottom with the kids, and I'm going, "Oh nothing, dear. It's nothing at all." And she said, "Something horrible's goin' on in my house! I demand to know what it is." "Oh, it was just a little mishap, dear." And, you know, every lie I'd ever told came out. And she comes down, and she's furious! She says, "Something's goin' on, I wanna know what it is." So we invite Mom in—now you see, and this of course, the family's sense of humor then with Barbara screaming, "What's going on?" Me saying nothing, these little traitors gave me away by starting to laugh and giggle. Mom started laughing and giggling, "Oh nothing, it's nothing." So Barbara comes in and I just have to tell her, "This is our life. This is how we've lived, Dad knocks us around, Dad's tough. It's been awful." And she said, "Why didn't you tell me?" And I said, "I should have. I should've told lots of people but I haven't." And that night, from that night I began writing *The Great Santini*. And that broke something in me that, what had to break is where I told myself the truth.

WE: How did you kids keep it bottled up?

JC: A military family.

WE: Okay, I understand that.

KH: But I think because we had each other to talk to and go through it together, I think that's what made the difference.

TC: Yeah, most of my brothers and sisters are very close, and growing up with them, even to this day, we're still very close. And it's been nice to have brothers and sisters that are very close, going through with what we did.

WE: One of the things when *The Great Santini*, the book, came out, people thought Pat exaggerated.

JC: I hear that all the time. I've always heard that. And I've told everybody, if you knew the truth, it was much worse than the book. And no one ever believes us.

KH: I thought he was the nicest character, my dad, in that book. I loved that dad. I wanted that dad.

JC: I prayed for that dad. [*laughter*]

WE: And your mom's reaction was, she didn't like the fact that Santini was the protagonist.

PC: She thought Dad was a dope. And I didn't know this until the book comes out, and she's furious it's called *The Great Santini*. She's furious it's not called, you know, *Mom*, and that she was not the central driving force in the book.

JC: *The Angel from Alabama*.

PC: *The Angel from Alabama*. I mean, you know, Mom really saw herself in this glorious Hollywood sort of way. Mom was very Hollywood, don't you think?

TC: She loved the fanfare over the movie.

PC: Oh yeah, and the flashiness, and even growing up, Mom was the type of mother made all of us feel ugly. And I once asked my sister Carol, I said, "Why don't we look as good as Mom?" My sister Carol said, "She married the beast." [*laughter*] But she was a glorious looking woman, took great pride in her beauty, and of course the rest of us, we're still in therapy trying to get over Mom and Dad.

TC: And Walter, I don't know if you know this but she's in *The Great Santini*. She's one of the characters, as is my younger brother Tom.

KH: He's talking about in the movie.

TC: *The Great Santini*. So she was in one of the scenes of the movie where her head is going back and forth like a ping-pong ball watching the kids play basketball, one side of the court to the other. And there's Blythe Danner and Robert Duvall, and she's right between 'em on the row right above them. So anyway, for us to go back and see the movie, we can see my mother, and we can also see my younger brother.

[*Mike Conroy joins the interview.*]

WE: All right, we want welcome another Conroy sibling, Mike, to the *Journal*, and so we've got everybody here but sister Carol. Sometimes you get the impression from your writings, Pat, that maybe everybody doesn't get along. But Jim, I understand your daughter got married last year, and everybody was there?

JC: Yes, it was called free drinks, Walter, they all showed up for it.

WE: Carol came down?

JC: Carol came down as well, and I think she had a great time. Kathy and I were just talking about it today. I think she had a great time there, and she really enjoyed it. But she has not been as close to the rest of us.

WE: Okay, she's not estranged from the family.

JC: No.

WE: No. And y'all keep in regular touch, all of you, even now?

JC: Weekly. [*laughter*] No.

KH: I don't know that you could call it regular touch, there's times when, for whatever reason, Carol has cut us off. So those periods have lasted a long time at different times in my life, adult life.

JC: I will hear from her at birthday, my birthday, and that's the only time I'll hear from her all year. And that's her choice. We've certainly tried to reach out to her.

WE: Mike, we've been talking really about *The Great Santini*, and I've heard your sister's and your brothers' reactions to the book. You wanna add anything about your reaction? How old were you when the book came out?

MIKE CONROY: I was about twenty-six.

WE: Okay.

MC: Yeah, it's all lies. [*laughter*] Dad and Mom were wonderful people. I don't know where Pat came up with this. [*laughter*] No, we support Pat very much.

WE: All right, I was gonna say 'cause that, what you had just said was a minority interpretation. Because I tossed out what a lot of people said about *The Great Santini*, the book, that it was all an exaggeration. Nobody could've lived in a world like that.

MC: Oh, it was pretty accurate. But we thought all families were like that. We thought all families moved every year or twice a year. So we had no other family to compare it with.

PC: Yeah, I didn't know that everybody wasn't goin' home after school getting beaten up. I just thought that's what a kid did. You know, you finish school, said goodbye to everybody on the bus.

WE: Surely you had childhood chums. Y'all didn't talk about, well I got—

JC: There were other military kids for the most part.

TC: You know, we moved every year.

MC: And also our childhood chums were— We moved to a new city. It takes a while to develop friends.

PC: You know, you can't get a chum right away. Kathy was one of the few I knew of all the kids that could make a friend. She'd always make one friend. Mike and Jim had such bad personalities they never made a friend during the entire school year. It took me a long time to make friends, and then we consistently moved every nine months. So, I didn't spend the night with somebody until I was a junior in high school. I mean, I never would have anybody spend the night with me, because I didn't want 'em to be thrown through a plate glass window by Dad.

MC: Now Pat, that was not true. In your college you brought a group of friends home to the house in Virginia, where—Remember the room?

PC: Oh, my God.

MC: I slept in an unheated basement, but your room you had to access through a closet.

PC: A closet for a dog. And I remember Mike—

MC: You had to get on your knees.

PC: —I had to get on my knees, and I had a guy that I played basketball with. And so I'd never been to this house, and they moved on me. And Mike says, "Hey, you wanna see your room?" And so he goes to his closet in this unheated basement, pulls open his clothes and there's a little doggie door for me and John DeBrosse to slip through. And as we're going through it, DeBrosse says, "Nice bedroom, Conroy." [laughter] And we still laugh. We had some of the most terrible bedrooms you've ever seen. And this was just part of the military life that we got used to.

JC: At least that bedroom had a great hiding place for us when Dad got mad. We would head down there.

PC: Oh, I mean, there was always a hiding place.

JC: Yeah.

WE: Kathy, Pat wouldn't have friends over for sleepovers. Did you?

KH: I did a couple of times, but it was always a dangerous situation. You had to be really careful because you never knew if my dad would be drunk or angry or upset or how he would come back into the house after work.

WE: Again I understand the military family; I understand the moving. But when you got to Beaufort, as close as you were to Gene Norris, he didn't suspect anything was going on?

PC: Well he did not. He later apologized to me. But I had an excuse. Mike had an excuse. All of us had an excuse as boys. You know, Dad really tore me—It was the time you fell outta the tree, Jim. And Jim was showing off as he always did as a kid and falls out of a tree on his head. So Dad had this one thing that tickled me and Carol, and we could not help it. Jim came in, he's crying, he's bleeding, and he comes in and Dad had this thing, he says, "All right, you better quit cryin'." And as soon as he would say, "You better quit cryin'," whap! He would backhand you. And, of course, as a little kid, he's cryin' ten times as hard. Mom's with him. So I cracked up. Dad threw a glass at my head, broke my head open, and it was just sort of seen that just, you did not know when it would break out. You had no idea when this was gonna happen. You know, Mom wanted me and Carol to sit nearest Dad 'cause we got the first hits, and she had us sit to the left 'cause that's how he hit. He was left-handed. So we would get the first hit. And Carol was dangerous because she irritated, you know, she could irritate Dad. But, but Carol was one of the great victims of the family also.

WE: Well, do all of y'all feel like victims?

KH: We were definitely victims, but I don't know that you felt like that at the time when you were going through it. I think more than anything I learned to sense danger, and when I walk into a room today, I can still feel it.

MC: Again, we thought all families were like this. Certainly when we visited up North, his brothers were the same way.

PC: I hated Dad's family. My God, they were horrible.

WE: The description of how they treated your mother, absolutely incredible. Mocking her accent, talkin' about Aunt Jemima, cookin', I mean, that—

PC: And they were too young—I don't even think y'all were born when those things happened.

JC: They did that when we visited.

PC: Really?

JC: Oh, yeah!

MC: Yeah. And we didn't visit there a lot, but they were not—

TC: When we went up there they'd mock our accents.

JC: None of them were very friendly towards any of us.

MC: No, no.

JC: And you have to remember back in the sixties or the late fifties, people didn't travel long distances, and we were living in Orlando or Virginia or D.C. or wherever, so they didn't come to visit us. So we would only see them once every few years, which was a blessing.

WE: And of course in the fifties and sixties, the stereotypes about the South were rampant.

JC: Correct.

WE: They're still out there but they were, but—

PC: With them it was just, you know, beyond a pale. When I wrote a book, my grandmother said, "Oh, I'm so glad you learned how to write books. I didn't even know you could read, Pat." So, this was a grandma I just didn't like, and I had this other grandma I adored. And I don't know how y'all liked Stanny, if she was crazy and—

KH: I loved her.

PC: —She came around.

WE: Stanny is Mrs. Conroy's mother. But what I was gonna say is you talk about the Chicago family, it sounds like your dad was reared in something of a dysfunctional household.

PC: Did y'all ever hear anything about that?

TC: I've heard from some of the uncles that they weren't raised in a real nice family either, that it was very dysfunctional. And that they were beaten and hit quite a few times. I've heard that from my uncles up there when I was there visiting. It certainly doesn't give my father the excuse, but—

WE: No, no, I wasn't trying to give an excuse—but in your characterizations of the visits there, and then also for example, your uncle who was the priest and the way he actually knocked people around. He knocked you around.

PC: He knocked me around. I found him knocking Tim around when I threatened to beat him up when I was in college. He slapped you at Great Falls in Virginia.

TC: Lord, love 'em.

JC: I think the difference was is that Tim deserved it. [*laughter*]

PC: But he was also the priest that comes down to deliver these terrible, horrible sermons. And remember what was it, at Tom's funeral?

TC: He said that Tim had died.

JC: My poor brother.

PC: When he said it again, he said "We're here together, the untimely death of . . ." he looks down and he says, "Uh, Timothy Conroy." And I looked back at Tim and I said, "Tim, I'm sorry you're dead."

TC: Right [*laughter*].

PC: "I thought it was Tom."

TC: There were groans all over the church when he said that, too, just—

PC: I mean, just, it went on. Then that was when Carol started throwing the softball straight in the air. It was just, it's always with the Conroys— A nightmare. This is why when Jim's beautiful daughter Rachel got married I thought—and my tension was not about anything that happened, but what could've happened.

JC: There was a lot of potential there, Walter. [*laughter*] It went over well. We were delighted with the wedding, but a lot of things could've happened.

WE: Had you explained to your wife what might have happened before? Like Pat hadn't told Barbara what kind of family she was marrying into. Was your wife prepared?

JC: Well we were kinda worried about her family a little bit too, Walter. [*laughter*] Nah, we've been married for over thirty years and so she's well aware of my brothers and sisters, and she knew my father too. And my mother. She wasn't worried about our family. She hasn't seen it as much.

WE: All right, let's go back to growing up years. And Pat, you've chronicled very much how your mother read to you and to Carol and made sure that you were, as Robert Penn Warren said, "bookish." You had a bookish upbringing. She read poetry to you. Did she do that with the rest of you all? Mike?

MC: No.

JC: No, she didn't.

MC: Reading was always encouraged. If you were reading you were pretty safe.

TC: I always thought it was because I was the fifth child, and she stopped reading after that, just going, "It wasn't worth it."

PC: I think this is one of the great surprises when *My Reading Life* came out 'cause Tim says, "She never read a word to me in my life." And, you know, Kathy, Mike, and Jim, they did not get read to. And it shocked me. And I'm sure it would shock Carol.

MC: Photographs of your children, you know, the first one you have a million photographs. Well I—

PC: We don't have a photograph of Tim growing up.

TC: She was exhausted by the time she got to me and Tom.

PC: I think so.

TC: She's saying, "Look at all the good things I did with the first two. None of it worked, so why do anymore?" [*laughter*]

KH: When I was in the fifth grade we lived in Omaha, Nebraska, and my mother had a hysterectomy, and I think that things for her became very different. She wasn't the same after that. And I think she became depressed and exhausted.

TC: That was a tough year, that year Pat went off to the Citadel as a freshman.

MC: You wouldn't believe how he complained about getting a college education.

PC: Free clothes.

MC: Yeah, free clothes, free food. He's bellyaching and—

PC: You listen to the University of South Carolina complaints. I complained about the plebe system, and they're thinking, oh clothes and food. Yeah. And Mom was cheap, and these kids did not have much going through Carolina. Mom would leave 'em out on a corner and, what, you said, Tim, that you didn't have a dorm room?

TC: Oh, sometimes when the day comes where the parents move in students to the university, and you see these loving parents take such care moving their sons and daughters. And transitioning these high school students to college. And my experience, Walter, was so different. My mom pulled up to the Student Housing Authority on Pendleton Street. I walked in, and they told me that I was on a waiting list for a dorm room. I came out, and I'm like, "Mom, I don't know what to do. I'm on a waiting list. I don't have a room to stay." And she unloaded my suitcases, and she said, "They'll work it out." And she drove off. [*laughter*]

WE: Well, did they work it out?

TC: No! I walked over to what was then the Campus Club South and told the bartender my story, and he died laughing. And introduced me to about thirty people that night, and I ended up staying in a foyer on Greene Street for about three weeks until my dorm room was open. And that was my introduction to the University of South Carolina.

JC: And he was one of the lucky ones. [*laughter*]

WE: Well, what was your experience, Jim?

JC: Oh, you know, they were all different, but the one thing is that our mother dropped him off at school. I left Hawaii, where I went to high school at, and came across the country after my father nearly knocked me through a sliding glass door. And my mother moved to Beaufort, and my father ended up moving to Atlanta, but they never visited us the entire time. I think my father came up my senior year at college and visited us for the first time. So he never saw a dorm room, never saw where I stayed. I had to go back and forth with my own things, but they just didn't visit. So it's just, uh, interesting parents.

WE: I'm just thinking in terms of time. Your dad retired, they divorced right after he retired. So you, the younger—

JC: She actually—

MC: We're from a broken home.

JC: She actually left Hawaii a year before he did, and for the reason being to fix up the house in Beaufort, which they had purchased from Pat. So, she was in Beaufort a year before, and when my father retired, or came across from Hawaii, retired in Beaufort and that's when she hit him with the divorce papers. Which she should've done that thirty years earlier, but—

WE: Kathy, you were the only child to testify in that case, weren't you?

KH: Yes. There was a wonderful judge at that divorce hearing, Judge Fanning.

PC: Yeah.

KC: Who said, "Kathy, I want you to tell me one story." And I did. And he said, "Thank you." And told me to go sit down. So I think he was probably the most wonderful man to me that day. My mom was crazy at that hearing and caused a huge scene. My mom required a lot of attention and the minute—

PC: Oh, come on, Kathy. [*laughter*]

KH: Before, um, Dad walked in to the courtroom, she said, "I think he's carrying a weapon. And there's gonna be trouble, and this is gonna be horrible." And they went back and talked to Judge Fanning, and Judge Fanning went up and talked to my dad and said, "Are you carrying a weapon?" And he said, "No."

PC: And they asked him marine to marine.

WE: Oh, okay.

PC: And, you know, that was good enough. And I think Dad broke down in tears, and we'd never seen—I didn't know Dad had an emotion that would include tears. Walter, one of the things I wanted my brothers and sister to talk about is the sister Carol thing. There's nothing I felt guiltier about in the book than writing about sister Carol. And we all know she's a wounded but powerful human being, and she exerts a powerful force on me and I think all of us.

TC: Well yeah, I'll tell one quick story.

WE: Go ahead.

TC: When I was a beginning teacher, I was working at a school who served kids with autism. And a lot of the students attending this school happened to be from New York. And so one holiday season, one Christmas season, I flew the kids back up to New York. About four kids. They were sixteen to eighteen years old, and once I got to New York City, met up with Carol. And I was supposed to stay with her, and this was really my introduction to New York City. I was really excited—and she spent very little time with me. I stayed in her place but we interacted just a very little bit. In one of the interactions she wanted me to tell my brothers and sisters that she did not want anything to do with them anymore. And I said, "Carol, you are gonna have to deliver that message. You're gonna have to tell them. Not me, I'm not the messenger." And so, and I think she was going through therapy at the time, and I think probably in her therapy, her therapist probably told her that was something she needed to do.

WE: Did she tell you she didn't want to interact with you anymore?

TC: She kinda told me by her lack of having anything to do with me while I was there.

WE: All right, did she deliver that message to you all? Or did it—

JC: Yeah, I think she—

KH: I think so.

PC: I think she, I think—

JC: It came across.

PC: It eloquently came across.

JC: We've given the same message to Tim, though. [*laughter*]

TC: Yeah, yeah.

JC: You can't shake 'em.

PC: No, Carol told me at my mother's funeral that her shrink, Naoko, knew more about our family than anybody else on earth. And I said, "Really? You know, I don't seem to remember meeting Naoko." And I said, "Carol, can we say that Naoko knows more about our family than anyone earth because of what she's heard from you?" And she said, "She says our family is toxic." And I said, "Carol, I've made a very good living on that particular idea, and I couldn't agree with you more." But I did not see Carol from the time of Mom's funeral until Tom committed suicide. And, you know, we did not see each other, have anything to do with each other at all, and she just told me she wasn't gonna see me, and she didn't. So now, the last time I saw her is generally when she shows up at celebrations, weddings, funerals.

MC: She's a good southern girl, no matter what.

PC: She always comes back for that. And usually makes her presence known.

WE: Well, but it sounds like the last show—when, at your daughter's wedding, Jim, that there weren't scenes.

JC: Yeah, there was potential but she was very good. She was on her best behavior, and I think she enjoyed it very much, so it was nice for us, nice for us to see that.

KH: I have some wonderful nieces that are Jim and Pat's children that were so gracious and loving and wonderful, along with my son who was at the wedding. They loved Carol so much and tried to have Carol participate in their lives. But it's really difficult to be able to stay in Carol's life because she's not able to.

WE: Okay. Well, one thing you mentioned earlier, both of you, is at the divorce your father crying and that this was the first time you'd really seen him give any kind of emotion or certainly of a sign of weakness, which he'd interpreted it as. You mentioned when Jim fell out of the tree and was crying, whopped you upside the head because that's what, "You should stop crying." And that really was the first time you saw him express any kind of emotion?

PC: Yeah, I can remember—can y'all remember another time you saw Dad crying?

JC: Yeah, Tom's death.

MC: Tom's death was awful.

JC: It broke him.

TC: It broke Dad.

PC: It broke Dad completely. Mike took care of Tom, and Mike performed heroically in that. But every once in a while Tom would go off, and he'd go off his meds, or he'd go off something. So when Tom committed suicide, that broke something in our family. But Dad was so broken up, cried so hard, cried for so long. I remember getting together the night we buried Tom and just say, "Okay, we now know Dad loves us. He just, he can't show it." But, you know, his reaction to Tom was so emotional, and it seemed so authentic, that we said, ah, okay.

KH: When we walked in the funeral home the night before the burial, I saw my dad's knees buckle from the outpouring of the community and family. It was so full of flowers. It was beautiful.

TC: And that's where we're blessed to be from South Carolina, because nobody rallies behind a family like South Carolinians do in a time of need.

PC: I've never seen anything like it. I mean, it just, it gets to us every time.

WE: Well, and you also talked about being inundated with the food, I mean, the very traditional South Carolina folks that were your neighbors that you didn't really know were your neighbors, all of a sudden they're on your doorstep. To help you through this.

PC: Yeah, they've done it every time. And it gets to us. And I think because we're a military family, it really gets to us. And how we have come to this state, and this state has come embrace our family. And it's a very nice thing. Although my brothers and sisters do have one thing they did that tickled me about my sister Carol. They talk about how Carol was gonna take the news when one of them gets to call her and say that Pat has died. [*laughter*] Okay now, she's grinning now.

WE: Mike, you're grinning the biggest.

MC: Well, I always want to see Carol happy. [*laughter*] I know that's gonna really tickle her, that call. And I've, I have some experience in making these phone calls, you know. And when Tom died, when Mom died, I had to call the others, tell 'em what happened. When Dad died, Kathy made the phone call, but that will be interesting to see Carol's reaction. Now she will come down for that funeral.

JC: Well, she's already prepared the eulogy.

MC: Actually, I didn't know if you knew Carol was gonna do your eulogy, Pat.

PC: I heard she wrote it twenty-one years ago. [*laughter*]

MC: She wrote a poem for Beowulf that's smaller than the poem Carol is writing. [*laughter*]

PC: And one time they were talking about calling Carol to tell Carol I died, and they—see, they did the dance of Carol as she dances around the room. And so the family I do think, when Kathy says the family humor has helped us. The dark one, the dark one kills us because his humor is, even for a Conroy, [*laughter*] I mean, his humor is out of sight.

TC: And it's dry.

PC: It's inhuman.

WE: Well, let's have an example. You keep talking about it, but I haven't heard it yet.

JC: I apologize for that, Walter. [*laughter*]

WE: Well? This is open mic time.

JC: I didn't prepare any lines.

MC: Tim did.

PC: Tim was ready. Tim was gonna—

TC: You know, I'd just like to say that my brother Mike sells real estate, my brother Jim is huge in the Mexican frozen food business, and—

KH: I do wanna tell ya, I, I saw my dad cry a lot after *The Great Santini* movie came out. Every time they showed the part about his death, he would have tears running down his face and tell me, "Tragic. This is tragic." [*laughter*] And it would be so fun to watch it, because it happened every time. "Pat made such a mistake. This is tragic." [*laughter*]

MC: He would be happy to know that there was another Great Santini book out.

PC: Yeah, he'd be signing it, you know.

MC: Mm-hm.

PC: You know, when I told him the name of this book when he was dying, *The Death of Santini*, he said, "Hey, great title. You really know how to make a guy feel good." [*laughter*]

WE: Any of you had a reaction from Carol to this book?

JC: Hum-um [*negative*].

WE: Okay.

KH: I have not.

WE: Okay.

JC: I don't know if she's read any of 'em after *The Great Santini*.

MC: She's read 'em.

JC: Yeah, I'm sure she—

PC: You think?

MC: Yeah.

JC: I can tell you my reaction.

MC: Well, she wrote me a little card about this book.

PC: What?!

MC: Yeah.

PC: Okay, this is Conroy secrets.

MC: Well, it was just one—it was a little postcard saying basically don't believe anything Pat said; it's all lies. Which I have to take it, a grain of truth anyway on that.

WE: Tim?

TC: Oh, I was just gonna say reading *The Death of Santini* was like beating myself up with a led pipe for every page. It was a tough read. My wife and I usually read Pat's books out loud to each other because we don't wanna be finished before the other, so we will usually take the time and read it to each other. And I tried to do this, we tried to do this with *The Death of Santini*, but my wife, Terrye, was crying so much that I could not get through. And it's a tough book.

PC: It's redemptive, but it's tough.

WE: Well I'd say even for a nonfamily member, yes, it is a tough book.

TC: But we're not victims, we're survivors. And you look at all of us and we survived.

WE: Well, and I'm still trying to fathom where you all got the sense of humor.

KH: It had to be from my dad.

WE: I was gonna say the Irish genes.

PC: Yeah, there's no— Mom did not have a sense of humor.

KH: My dad was so funny. But we didn't know that when we were children.

JC: And it's also gallows humor, you know.

WE: Well, what about Stanny, she seems to—your maternal grandmother—she seems to be an incredible individual who certainly was lighthearted and—

KH: I think she was a storyteller.

PC: Did she live with y'all a lot?

KH: Enough to why I know why you're laughing, yes.

PC: I would call Stanny when Mom had her hysterectomy, when I was a freshman at the Citadel. And, you know, the Citadel doesn't encourage you to call home much. And because my family's extraordinarily cheap whenever—and I would get this with Mom: "There's a collect phone call from Pat Conroy." And I'd hear from my mother, "We don't know a Pat Conroy." [*laughter*] And I'd have to say, "Mom! Will you answer the phone?" And, but Stanny had a drinking problem, and I don't know what that was like for y'all. You know, up in Omaha, Nebraska, but I would get Stanny on the phone, and she would go—she'd had some drinks—she would say, "Your momma's dyin'. She's just dyin'. You gonna be down there at the Citadel doin' nothin' while she's just up here a-dyin'. And you gonna have to come home and take care of these children." And, and that was a promise I made to Mom.

WE: Alfred's giving me the windup. What I'd like to do is to let each one of you have a last word before we sign off. And since, Tim, you're seated to my right, I'm gonna ask you to go first.

TC: It's been a journey with all of my brothers and sisters, and really I think because of Pat's writing and his work, it allowed us to have truth and illumination of the pain and suffering we went through. And it has proven to be just redemptive. His work has helped us. I think it's brought us closer. It's made us stronger and when you read his works, all of them, from his fiction to his nonfiction, he always exposes the truth.

WE: Okay. Kathy?

KH: I'm very grateful for the book *The Great Santini*. The book, as painful as it was when it came out, helped my dad reinvent himself. I know he did it as competition, but he ended up loving all of us and showing us.

WE: Jim?

JC: I wanted to make a comment about my father. Pat spoke of him as never having said that he loved any of us. My father told me he loved me constantly. [*laughter*] And I think it was just the other brothers and sisters. And now that you've met them, Walter, you probably understand a little bit why he didn't love them as much. But he certainly did say that to me. Thank you.

WE: Okay. So, you and Bobby Joe. [*laughter*]

JC: Well, yes, I would be just like Bobby Joe. I've enjoyed all of Pat's books. He's been a great writer, in each one he's gotten better and better. Pat has involved all of us in all of his books, movies, or whatever. He's been a fabulous brother, as have my other brothers and sisters as well.

WE: Okay. All right, Mike?

MC: Pat's spoken this at many times that Dad had a great second act. You know, he was real hard on us when we were young, but as we got to be adults we basically told Dad, "You either change or you're not gonna be in our lives." And to his credit he changed 100 percent and became a great grandfather, and a nice person to be around. But we just weren't gonna put up with the attitude we had to put up with as kids.

WE: Okay. Pat?

PC: You know, just sitting here in this interview has made me wish I had a much better group of brothers and sisters [*laughter*] to share the journey that Tim talks about. No, you know, the one thing that I have loved about my writing career is throughout everything, I cannot explain this, I cannot understand it all, but there was something about the Conroys: they end up adoring each other. And, I can say violence. I can say this. I can say tragedy. We've all had tragedy. We've all gone through this, but you hit a mother lode of pure love when you're dealing with the Conroy family. And I think this has been the theme of my life, my work, my affection, and my writing in general.

WE: Well, I'd like to thank Kathy Harvey, Tim Conroy, Jim Conroy, Mike Conroy, and Pat Conroy for being with us today on *Walter Edgar's Journal*.

If I had to sum it up in one word I'd say, *Wow*. Growing up with the Great Santini was not easy for anyone. And in the past author Pat Conroy has often been accused of exaggerating the incidents in his childhood, but listening to his four siblings discuss with him what it was like to grow up with the Great Santini makes it quite clear. And at one point I think every one of them said, "Pat didn't exaggerate. He didn't even get close to what life was like." And it's really hard to imagine what that life was like for these young people. I need to point out that the gathering of the five Conroy children is actually a first time that they have all been together to publicly discuss what their childhood was like. And at times it was not easy, but tough questions, tough issues and a family history were handled with grace and with a sense of humor.

A Conroy Family
Roundtable

After hearing the SCETV-Radio broadcast of the February 28, 2014, conversation, the five Conroy siblings agreed to have a public conversation at the South Carolina Book Festival. This conversation, moderated by journalist and editor Aïda Rogers, was held on May 12, 2014, before a packed house at the Columbia Metro Convention Center.

AïDA ROGERS: And now is when I introduce this wonderful family, except that I don't really know them either. I've met Tim and Pat, and I know they're lovely, and I'm gonna have them introduce themselves. And I think if you just want to say a little bit about who you are, what you do, what you had for lunch, just whatever will bring us all together.

TIM CONROY: My name is Tim Conroy and I'm a former special education teacher. I had the burden of being the youngest of the siblings up here and so as the fifty minutes play out, you'll probably understand my burden even more. [*laughter*] I'm married to a wonderful woman, Terrye, and she's sitting over there, and she is my rock and love of my life. [*applause*] Beat that.

JIM CONROY: I think the fifty minutes are already over. [*laughter*] I'm brother Jim, Pat's favorite brother by the way. [*laughter*] I live in Charlotte, and I work for a company called Ruiz Foods out of

California, and I'm in sales. And this is my wife over here, Janice. She's got her hand halfway up. She's a little more— [*applause*] She's a little more embarrassed than Terrye. It's on you, Kath.

KATHY HARVEY: My name is Kathy. I'm the youngest daughter, youngest sister, if any of you are confused as to what order I am. I'm married to Bobby Joe Harvey, and I have one son, named Willie. I'm a registered nurse. And I live in Beaufort, and I've been working for the Marine Corps for the last twenty-one years. [*applause*]

MIKE CONROY: My name's Mike Conroy. I'm the, we're sitting in order of age so not to confuse you. My sister Carol would be here [*gestures*], but she lives in New York City—

PAT CONROY: And that's not why she's not here. [*laughter*]

MC:—and she doesn't talk to Pat. I'm a retired state employee. I do real estate with Exit Real Estate Solutions. Let's see, my wife is sitting on the first row there. Jean, stand up Jean. [*applause*] Jean is a schoolteacher. She's just completing her forty-first year teaching in the public schools. [*applause*] She's been at Joseph Keels for the last thirty-one years off of Parklane Road. And she said if I said anything negative about her, she would kill me. [*laughter*] She's a wonderful person. On you, Pat.

PC: My name's Pat Conroy. I am the lucky oldest brother. As the group just introduced itself in such flowery, glowing, glowing terms, I feel lucky to be born with this tribe because I think I survived our tumultuous family history because I love my brothers and sisters. And my job was easy: Mother said, when the beast goes crazy, my job was to get them out of the way. Now I have no idea if they remember this or not, but Mom and I would scout out each house to find hiding places for when Dad blew. When Vesuvius went off, we had one great house in Spring Valley Drive in Alexandria, Virginia, with the best hiding places. We had another place where there was a tree right outside the house, where I could flip them up the tree, and we had closets. We had everything else. But my job was to shepherd them like a dog to that whenever Dad went off. So I felt very protective of my brothers and sisters in growing up. And, you know, here's what's amazing to me. I've written about this, the nuttiness in my family, the craziness of my family, but they grew up to be these nice people. I do not know how Mom and Dad did this. I don't know how they survived their childhood, but they did it with grace, and they've all become really good citizens of the realm and good people to have living in your town and good neighbors. And somehow my mom and dad did something right while doing something horrible at the same time. Naturally I was the only one who noticed Mom and Dad were doing things wrong, except my sister Carol. But these four seemed to come through great to me. But they will tell you their story, and I will not. [*laughter*]

MC: It was all due to your influence. [*applause*]

AR: I thought I'd just sort of jump in because Tim has been my spy into the family. He gave me this long list of things I could ask about and what I learned is that y'all have your own vocabulary, your own language in the Conroy family. There's *guts football, the youngest of the boys;* there's *goosh* and I want to ask y'all to do the *goosh,* if you don't mind.

PC: Okay, brother Jim invented *goosh* in our family. Jim, since you're the inventor of it, please tell them what it means.

JC: I have no idea what he's talking about. [*laughter*] My father used to, you know, hit us on occasion. You know, I think he probably hit Pat more than anybody else, and that was probably earned. [*laughter*] But he only hit us once a year, which is a joke, and, anyway, I used to say that, Dad would come in and, *goosh,* he would hit us again. *Goosh, goosh, goosh.* And Pat just always loved hearing that so it's just reminded him of my father so much. [*laughter*]

AR: I thought it was some kind of dance you did with *goosh.* I thought there was a movement.

JC: Obviously Aïda you have not seen Conroys dance. And you would not want to see us dance, there was nothing we did other than that. It was just when we were being hit, so—

AR: Well, on a positive note, who, who did—?

MC: That's as positive as it gets. [*laughter*]

PC: Good luck. That was the positive part.

AR: I do wanna say this: I've read *The Death of Santini,* and I loved it. And I remember your line about how you don't dance, but your parents were great jitterbuggers.

PC: Yeah.

AR: Can't you demonstrate? I mean, they didn't teach you?

MC: No!

PC: Can you dance, Tim? Tim can dance.

AR: Would you like to—?

TC: No, I really, I really can't dance. Maybe if Jim would say *goosh!* [*laughter*] But, you know, my father was a great dancer, and my mom could dance, but none of that came down to us.

PC: They didn't teach us.

TC: Yeah, they did not teach us anything. Anything! You know, I don't think my father owned a hammer, a screwdriver, any tool. I don't remember him sitting down with me and saying, "Son, let me teach you something." We were kids of the fifties. We observed and did not participate.

MC: But Dad did. He was sports-oriented.

TC: Yeah.

MC: And then he taught us how to bat and shoot a basketball. He was left-handed so all of us bat left-handed. [*laughter*] He didn't care if you were right-handed.

JC: Do you bat left-handed?

TC: No, I bat right-handed.

PC: We were right-handed.

MC: Yeah.

AR: Oh, you were trained to be left-handed?

MC: We were trained to bat with the left-hand.

MC: That's how he would teach us, you know, how he did it. So I'm a left-handed batter. I think you were left-handed?

PC: [*nods yes*]

JC: Right-handed.

MC: Right-handed?

JC: Yeah.

TC: I was younger, and he didn't teach me anything. [*laughter*]

AR: So that explains the cake, the notes about the cake, if you wanted a piece of cake.

MC: Oh, yeah, the cake.

AR: Who wants to talk about that?

KH: I'll talk about the cake.

JC: She jumped in.

KH: My mom would make cakes out of cake mixes. She was not famous for her great cooking.

MC: What? [*laughter*]

KH: And she would hide the cakes after she made them, but when you're with seven kids in a house and really most of the houses were really small, it wasn't hard to find this cake. So we would cut a piece with our left hand and it was my dad who would get in trouble for it [*laughter*] as we stood there silently smiling.

AR: I noticed that y'all had methods for survival and, and a little bit of revenge, right, in that household.

MC: Yeah, getting money was one thing. There was very little money. So Dad would come home and put his change on the top of the dresser. Well by the morning, there'd be nothing there because each kid would go up and take a little. If you took a little, he wouldn't notice, but when you had seven kids, it didn't take much. It just disappeared. And to his credit he never figured it out. [*laughter*]

AR: Could you compare notes on who got the most money? Or did you confront each other with that?

PC: No, no. Here's what has happened with us, with money, is Mom and Dad screwed all of us up with money terribly. We simply had none, and I tell this, nobody believes me except them—

[*sounds of crying infant in audience*]

You can leave babies here. Don't worry about the baby. We were seven kids; we got it. [*applause*]

And so, you know, this thing with my mom, when I was in Beaufort High School in 1963, my allowance was a dime a week. And I said, "Mom, you know, my God, I want to go out. I go crazy." And she said, "Your father and I figure you won't be attractive to gangs [*laughter*] if you don't have any money." I said, "You know, Mom, all gangs, when they hear about that big ten cents a week, they're always trying to recruit me." [*laughter*] And when I went to the Citadel, it was ten dollars a month that she would send me, and then she'd write me letters: "If you have any money left over, please send it back. We're having a tough time." All of us got affected by this. Is that proper? So my brother Mike, who's the meanest member of the family, called everybody by the name of what we became because of mom's stinginess. And Mike loved the Aesop fable "The Grasshopper and the Ants." Okay, if you remember that fable, you know the grasshopper is playing all summer. He's fiddling and dancing, and the ants are working their behinds off. And so wintertime comes, and the ants have put up stuff, and the grasshopper comes starving, crawling up in the snow, but he didn't work during the summer, so he knocks on the ants' door, and they're eating their food. So the grasshopper begs to get in, and the ants say, "No, no, no, you did not work during the summer so we're not gonna let you in." So they let the grasshopper die of starvation and freezing outside. Mike has all of us in the family named either grasshopper or ant.

TC: Grasshopper. [*laughter*]

PC: Okay, but with a caveat. Tim's very proud he's a grasshopper. The mean ants say he's a grasshopper when it comes to him and Terrye, but he is an ant when it comes to buying gifts for us. [*laughter*]

TC: Absolutely.

PC: Okay, then we have—

MC: He's a piss ant.

PC: A piss ant. [*laughter*] Then we have Mike, who very proudly considers him the great ant of the family. And Mike and Jean, they are millionaires. They have more money than anybody in the family, and they will both deny—Jean's sitting there, "Oh, my God, no!" And they own half of South Carolina in acreage. Kathy is also an ant, and she's very proud of it. Now Jim is an ant wannabe. And the reason he cannot be an ant— He'd love to be an ant.

JC: I wish I was an ant. [*laughter*]

PC: He married a grasshopper.

MC: A grasshopper. [*laughter*]

JC: And I have two grasshopper kids.

PC: Okay, Carol Ann is a grasshopper without money.

MC: Carol Ann is a cricket, and she only comes out at night.

PC: [*laughter*]

KH: Can you guess who's the Jurassic grasshopper sitting at the table?

MC: Pat, the Jurassic grasshopper. [*laughter*]

PC: See, that's the positive part of the family.

MC: Who married—He's married to an ant over there.

PC: Wait a minute. But my ant wife that I married, she was an ant when I married her. She is going through a change of species, a metamorphosis. [*laughter*]

AR: We'll move right along to Kathy, the only girl at this table. What's it like to be a girl surrounded by these boys?

KH: For me it was wonderful. We moved a lot as all of you know who have read Pat's books. I always had someone to play with. All of us were really close in age, so there was always a playmate. Growing up with my father as a girl was, it was as if the females were invisible. My dad encouraged nothing, and you were the housekeeper, helper. And with Santini I learned quickly after watching glasses being thrown at Pat, to be quiet and not to laugh. And I learned that at a very early age.

AR: And I understand you don't laugh out loud even now. Is that true, or is that Tim just feeding me stuff?

KH: No, I still don't.

AR: So that's, that's like your biggest scar, biggest scar from growing up, or should I ask?

KH: Oh, I think that's probably the scar you hear.

AR: Who wants to talk about Most Like Dad, *MLD*? [*laughter*] This is one of those little catch phrases they have.

PC: This is called annually the MLD award, and the brothers get together. We decide which one of us has been Most Like Dad during the year. What is horrifying about this competition: it's close. [*laughter*] It is close. And, you know, and it is killing me personally that each year I'm growing more and more like my father. I even look in the mirror, and I say, "Good God Almighty! You are so ugly. You look just like Dad!" [*laughter*] And it is also the way I talk and my gestures, and everything seems to be getting more like him where I used to pray that I was adopted. That was my prayer, but there's no question. I was not adopted. But this Most Like Dad, we'll get together, and now Tim always loved it. He's loving this. Tell 'em, Tim, where you come out in the group.

TC: Oh, I think that all of us can exhibit a tone, a reaction that connects us with that feeling of MLD. Although I think I do it less. [*laughter*]

MC: I don't know what you're talking about.

TC: Than some!

AR: Do you have the control to stop yourself when you catch yourself pulling an MLD?

JC: No.

PC: Three of us do. [*laughter*]

AR: Do you want to name names or just—?

PC: Oh, here, what we have not told you is, Jim, do you want, maybe wanna, you know, take over here? There is one of us who wins the MLD contest every year, hands down, no question about it. Jim, go ahead. [*laughter*]

JC: First of all, I want to ask Aïda a question, do you have any friends? [*laughter*]

AR: One.

JC: I mean, yes, they've said that I'm MLD, which I think is very unfair. But to be nice to my brothers and sister, they said that at times they are like my father as well, and it's no compliment, trust me. So I would argue that case.

AR: I just want to ask the audience, how many of you heard Walter Edgar's interview with the family? Several of y'all.

MC: Oh, that's so sad. [*laughter*]

AR: It seemed very father focused, and I thought we could talk about your mom some. Is there a Most Like Mom? Y'all don't do that, or are there so many boys?

JC: No.

AR: Would you like to continue with that?

JC: No. [*laughter*]

PC: Kathy, you go ahead.

JC: Just tell 'em you're Most Like Mom. They'll believe it. [*laughter*]

KH: My mom was a beautiful woman, who was very cheap and self-centered and all about herself. And it was very difficult to grow up in that kind of household because then we also had Don, who was crazy and mean.

MC: That's as positive as it gets.

MC: Yeah, my mother was a saint—[*laughter*]—who loved me more than the other kids, and it's obvious.

JC: When we were young, we grew up, and my mother saved us so many times, and as we were little, we didn't notice her flaws. We thought she was a wonderful human being, and she was. She jumped in and stopped my father from hitting us and stopped fights, and she had a lot of great qualities. But later in life, I think some of her other qualities came out, and it's harder for us to identify with her. She was a good person and was, you know, married to a monster and had seven kids, so it must have been an incredibly difficult life for her.

PC: Six monstrous kids.

JC: She, she had seven monster kids.

TC: Okay, to be fair to her, living with my father just wore her out, and she broke, literally broke. And I think she went through a period of time after, right before the divorce and after the divorce, where she was really trying to discover who she was. And she kinda left everybody at that point, you know, and she became not a mother. She kind of stopped doing that, but she kinda had to do that to really discover who she was.

MC: You know, one thing about Mom is in the divorce. At that time in the early seventies when a military wife divorced the husband, they did not get any of the retirement. So the husband didn't owe them anything. That's since changed, but when she got the divorce, all she got was whatever the child support was from the kids who stayed at home. So when I was in college starting in 1970, my allowance was forty dollars a month. Now realize at that time, a meal ticket cost forty-three dollars, which lasted about three weeks. So when Pat was saying we didn't have any money, we didn't have any. Fortunately I had great friends. I had a friend from Orangeburg. He fed me my junior year, so fortunately all of us had great friends who helped us out.

TC: He was a great shoplifter also. [*laughter*]

MC: Lies! Don't believe it, just lies.

KH: Also, during those times women did not tell. My mom never told her sisters that she was being abused. So when my mom left my father, it was a shock not just to friends but to her family. And a lot of her family did not stand there by her side because they loved my dad, and they didn't believe her.

MC: That was the one thing that we couldn't believe. My father was the best person to every niece and nephew. They loved him to death 'cause he was a great guy. That was when we all got outta college, we said we don't have to put up with this. In your retirement, don't come around. He totally changed. Pat calls it "the greatest second act." But when he saw that he was losing his kids and they didn't wanna be there, he totally changed, and he became a nice guy and a great grandfather to all his grandkids.

AR: I have to ask about your Aunt Marge in the book. She had the great arm. She threw the softball, and I'm picturing this battle-ax. And, do y'all wanna describe her? 'cause she's fearsome.

MC: Yeah, she's a nun.

AR: Right, I know.

MC: She's a Catholic nun.

JC: Didn't we have a Most Like Marge contest? [*laughter*]

MC: Cute, cute.

JC: My sister.

PC: Kathy, go ahead.

MC: You kinda look like her. [*laughter*]

KH: Yeah, we actually did have a Most Like Marge. Whenever they would get mad at me, that would be what they would say, "I think you remind me of Aunt Margie," who was very terrifying. And those of us who were in Chicago when I was in the fifth grade—We were moving to Omaha, Nebraska. Mike and I and my sister, Carol, were in the middle of an Irish Catholic restaurant, and my aunt had had too much to drink and got angry with us and started screaming in the middle of this restaurant, and it was horrible. And she left to go to a convent a couple of blocks away. And we had my father, who came to pick us up, and we were terrified to get into the car because his first question was, "Where's Aunt Margie?"

MC: She was so mad at us, she couldn't finish the meal. And we're thinking, we're dead; we're absolutely dead. My father was very cool about it, which amazed us. We got back to his relatives. Well, Marge had beaten us back, and his relatives just went nuts at us, and Dad said, "Get up to your room!" So, and they were screaming, so we were up there thinking, we're dead. Dad came up there and said, "We'll leave tomorrow. Don't worry about it." You know, so that was part of him changing.

AR: I'm curious about when y'all started realizing that your upbringing was not normal?

MC: I was about twenty-six. [*laughter*] You know, we lived on military bases, we thought everybody, every family was like this.

PC: I thought everybody went home at night, whatever base we were on, and later the dad would come in and beat 'em up. So I just thought that was happening to everybody 'cause it's the only child-hood you ever live. You have nothing to compare it to, you know. I just thought, "Okay, they're gettin' beat up, I'm gettin' beat up. This is what happens when you're a kid." And I imagine even girls and boys who are sexually abused don't know that's not happening everywhere. And here's what my big surprise has been since I wrote about this, is that people, when they come up to me at signings, they tell me stories that are many times much worse than the ones I write down. And it has astonished me from the time I started writing that they've had worse stories. And none of them had brothers and sisters as bad as I have. [*laughter*] But, you know, sometimes the parents can do things I could not believe.

MC: The first time I really knew that our family was unusual was when I read *The Great Santini*. [*laughter*] All of a sudden, I go, "Wow!" So that really shined a light on it.

AR: But I'm guessing if you went to your friends' houses, you saw a different kind of mom, a different kind of dad. I mean, I know you traveled so much.

MC: Base, military base.

AR: Right, were they the same or—?

PC: You know, nobody ever invited me to spend the night.

MC: There's a reason for that, Pat. [*laughter*]

PC: In fact Mike and Jean won't even have me spend the night, and they live in Columbia, and I've gotta get a hotel. But I never had a friend. We'd move every year. And I'd go in. I didn't know anybody. You know, Mom would always say that we were doing it for the Marine Corps, and you're learning how to meet people, and she would always tell me, "Go up to people in high school and say, 'Hi, my name is Pat Conroy. I'm new around here. Can you show me a few of the ropes?'" And I'd say, "Mom, I'm a teenager." But I just didn't know what a normal family was like. And I'm not sure I do now because I will talk to people 'cause all of you have some crazy in the family. It's interesting to me, we have Carol, who is one of the great wounds of our family. We have Tom, who should be sitting there, is the great wound of our family 'cause he committed suicide. And we always have these things, but we have that way of laughing through darkness and horror that has become the Conroy way. But Carol should be telling her part of the story. I think it would be a different part.

MC: Carol's the cricket in the room.

AR: Well I wanted to ask about Carol. I was fascinated by the funeral scene in *The Death of Santini* and the whole ball of tears that kept going up in the air. I guess that was very noticeable to everybody in the church, this ball of tears that she'd toss up?

PC: Now people think I exaggerate in my books.

MC: What? [*laughter*]

PC: This is after the suicide of my brother, Tim, and Carol—

MC: Tom. Tom.

KH: Tom.

PC: Tom, excuse me. [*laughter*]

MC: Tim's over there. [*laughter*]

JC: We always hoped it would be Tim. We loved Tom more. [*laughter*]

TC: Talk about the card, I mean—

MC: Freudian slip.

PC: Freudian slip.

JC: We did like Tom more.

PC: My Uncle Jim, who did the mass there, kept sayin'—[*laughter*] I'm just thinking of the funeral, all during the funeral, he referred to the suicide of my brother Tim. So Tim was sitting behind me, and I said, "Tim, I'm so sorry you killed yourself." [*laughter*] "I thought that was Tom." And I can't believe I did the same thing, please excuse me.

MC: The program had Tim.

TC: Even Tim was in the program, in the card.

PC: That's right, I forgotten that. The program had Tim.

JC: Yeah, the program. We got there, we were at the funeral home.

PC: It was Tim's death.

TC: Only our family.

PC: But it's the Conroy family, so we're not surprised at that. But this did surprise us, Carol was supposed to be sitting with the family, and she decided—She leaps out of the car. Bobby Joe, who is Kathy's redneck husband, was the leader of the pallbearers. And so, Carol leaps out and says, "I will not be refused. I'm gonna bear my brother's body to the last, to the grave. And I, because I am a woman, but I am strong and I am—," you know. And she burst into that song, and then she tells the funeral director. Kathy, didn't he tell Bobby Joe to go sit down?

KH: Yes.

PC: So Carol takes the thing, and in our family Tim is guilty of this. When we carried Mom, and Tom was, you know—The rest of us guys are sitting there carrying Mom, and Tim and Tom leave the thing, and these are heavy. I don't know if you all have ever done this. And Tim would go, "How you doing?" Tim would be hugging people on the side. Tom would be hugging people over on the side, and Jim and I were in the back, and we're goin' to our knees. [laughter] But Carol at Tom's funeral, she told Father Jim he could not mention the fact that Tom was mentally ill because Tom was the sanest of all of us. Is that not true?

TC: Yes, that's true.

PC: Okay now take it from what we saw from then. Carol's over on the other side with the pallbearers.

TC: It's hard to tell this story and give it its justice because Pat's written about this so well and with so much humor. But Father Jim, my uncle, the worst public speaker in the universe of Catholic priests, is screwing up every detail of Tom's service. And, he mentions fifty times Tom was mentally ill, and every time Carol hurls up the ball of tears.

PC: She'd been collecting them.

MC: The Kleenex.

TC: The tissues.

PC: Yeah, and she wouldn't throw them away.

TC: And so it gets bigger and bigger and bigger.

PC: It was like this [gestures]. [laughter]

TC: And it becomes a basketball going up through the pews and we looked back and it's like watching a tennis match. Everybody in the church is going up, down, and it's like it's unbelievable. [laughter] You wanna add?

JC: There was no Most Like Father Jim contest. [*laughter*] I just wanna make that clear. No, it was a terrible funeral for everybody but my uncle that was up there. He was doing so many things that were horrible, and Carol was doing things, and she had to talk, and that was awful as well. But I remember my uncle up there at the thing saying—Tom attended USC. And we're all proud Gamecocks, except for Pat, and so we would hear this, and he would say, my uncle the priest giving this eulogy, he said, "Tom attended the University of Southern Colorado." [*laughter*] I reached over for the napkins or whatever from Carol and threw it up in the air. It's just, he was such an idiot. It was so sad. [*laughter*]

KH: The one thing that was wonderful about Tom's funeral is we had wonderful community support. We had the whole town of Beaufort come out and help us through that. And it was just unbelievable when we walked into the funeral home. It was filled with flowers. When we went to Pat's house after the funeral, there was so much food that people had brought.

MC: But for a Conroy event, it really went off pretty well. [*laughter*]

AR: Which leads me to Christmas with the Conroys. I understand that's a good question to ask, and I don't know why.

TC: Well, I think the early days—

PC: Who has been questioned the most, do you think? In this panel?

MC: Tim. He set up these questions.

PC: Go ahead, Tim.

TC: Since I'm the most generous Conroy, spending the most money on presents and—No, really, talking about Christmas when I was a kid, and I remember being so excited about Christmas morning and all the presents around the tree. And I know that it was a morning that the dawn brought new promise. And something always would happen to kinda mess it up. You know how Christmas mornings are. But I remember my sister Carol would strategically hoard her presents and not open 'em. And so while everybody else was sort of pacing and taking turn at opening their presents and responding to their presents, Carol would make sure that she would have her pile left and wait to the very end, and then be very insufferable about opening these presents very slowly, and she just loved that ritual. And I know y'all remember more about that so, go ahead, Kathy, fill in the—

KH: My sister Carol loved presents more than anyone I've ever met.

MC: Except for Kathy.

KH: But it's really difficult to watch someone keep opening presents when you're done. And it became very painful each Christmas, but we did get better about it and try to slow down. But she was hilarious.

MC: Mom made Christmas very special. It was like most families of the fifties and sixties. There was no money but there were always plenty of presents on Christmas morning. So as kids, we were real excited. There's only one other person I know that loves presents as much as Carol, and that's my sister Kathy. [laughter]

KH: But I open very fast.

AR: Well in this family full of boys, you had to get girl toys I guess. And did these boys torment you for the girl toys you got?

MC: Who wants to play with girl toys?

KH: No, no, everybody shared.

AR: Oh, okay. You want to talk about Christmas dinner? I know your mom was not a cook. I'm just wondering what a clan of Irish Catholics from Chicago and another group from Alabama might have for Christmas or Thanksgiving?

MC: My mother was a wonderful cook. [laughter] Pat, being a gourmet cook, never appreciated her food. But we knew what day of the week it was by what we had for dinner.

PC: Tell 'em. Tell 'em, Mike.

MC: One day would be spaghetti, Sawyer's packet spaghetti.

PC: Italian night. [laughter]

MC: Friday, everybody knows who's lived in the south, fish sticks. Pat ridicules me to this day because I still like fish sticks. [laughter]

TC: Hit-and-run Saturday.

MC: Hit-and-run. When Mom got tired of cooking. "What are we having for dinner, Mom?" "Hit-and-run." That means you went to the kitchen, you made your dinner, and you cleaned up. But a routine was after you ate your meal, "Mom, that was a great dinner." You know, no matter what we had, that's what you always told her.

AR: And chores in this house? Did you wash your own? Did y'all take turns? I mean, were y'all good kids emptying the trash?

MC: You cleaned your area. But Jim, you need to say some more. [*laughter*] Pat never cleaned up anything.

TC: No, I love the story about my brother Tom. Tom and I, for long parts of my life, we slept in the same bed. He was three years younger, and often we had to share rooms. And making the bed was a mandatory function in the house, and so Tom and I would try, and we kinda perfected this, we would try to make the bed while still in it. And so, we'd pull up the sheet and pull up the bedspread and then we'd slip out the sides and kinda straighten it up.

AR: I'm gonna let y'all go around the table. I sent y'all this question, you might dislike it, but I know you can go with it. Pick one word to describe each other.

MC: Wonderful. [*laughter*] We're very supportive and couldn't ask for better brothers or sisters. [*applause*] They're such a quick-thinking family.

AR: Y'all lettin' him have the last word?

PC: Okay this is so personally nauseating to me. [*laughter*] This was wonderful. I have made a living out of describing our family life. It is less than wonderful. Now if you wanna see how our family life really was, look at my brother Jim's expression right now. [*laughter*]

JC: *Goosh!*

PC: And I can't help it, Mike's sayin' Mom was a wonderful cook. The worst cook that ever turned on fire in an American kitchen. [*laughter*] And Mike, can you imagine eating fish sticks?

MC: And pork and beans!

PC: Mike's freezer is still filled with fish sticks. We ate chicken pot pies. You ever eaten that crap? [*laughter*] I ate four million chicken pot pies growing up, and I had not seen them in years until I opened Mike's freezer, and they're loaded with chicken pot pies. And he did think Mom was a great cook. Spaghetti night, Italian night. I hated pasta. I moved to Rome. The reason I hated pasta—Mom would cook it, I don't know what she did with it, I think it was not enough water, but it looked like an octopus when it would come out. [*laughter*] And she would cook these down so long, she would put it in a colander, and it was a lump you could pick up with your hand. [*laughter*] And Mom would pick it up with her hands after it cooled off. She'd walk it over to the cutting board, and we would get slices. [*laughter*] And she would cut off nine slices of pasta.

MC: You're making my mouth water. [*laughter*]

PC: And Mike has driven me crazy by saying she was a fabulous cook. It's driven me nuts. But anyway, go ahead gang, Tim—

MC: Tim alluded to our bedrooms and that, that may—

TC: Oh, you wanna talk about when y'all slept outside or in the basement?

MC: It was seven kids. We always had a small house. Jim and I shared a room in Pensacola, Florida. It was a screened porch. [*laughter*] When it rained, we got wet. [*laughter*]

JC: Rain? It was cold! [*laughter*] Pensacola, Florida, was not Miami. The winter was horrible.

MC: Pensacola has about the same weather as Columbia.

PC: That wasn't the worst place.

MC: Oh, yeah.

JC: No.

MC: Omaha.

PC: I come back from the Citadel. As y'all know, I enjoyed my freshman year at the Citadel a great deal. [*laughter*] Okay, I feel like I've been half beaten to death. Mom just had a dreadful hysterectomy. It has been the most horrible year of my life. I get back there, and so I'm talking to Mom, begging them to let me leave school. "They're monsters down there, oh, I'm faced with monsters." And Dad says, "Shut up!" But I finally have to go to bed, and I said, "Mom, where's my new bedroom?" She said, "You're sleeping downstairs with Jim, Kathy, and Mike." And Tim was a baby then, I think you were sleeping with Mom and Dad. So anyway, it's in Omaha, Nebraska. It's ten below zero. I've never been in below zero weather in my life. I open this door, and it was like stepping into a freezer. And I cut on the light and I am cussin' goin' downstairs, I said, "Jesus, God Almighty! This is child abuse." So I get down there, and all three of these little jerks are sitting there already in their beds.

MC: There are no heaters. It's an unheated basement. We said the last one in has to turn out the light, which is at the top of the stairs. [*laughter*] Once that light goes off, you can't see your hand in front of your face.

PC: And so I go down there, and they're blowing air, you know, they're blowing to the roof.

MC: Because we're laughing so hard.

PC: And I said, "God! This is where you sleep? I'm calling the child abuse hotline." And I've never been that cold. And then of course I get in my underwear or whatever, I think it was underwear. I don't think we had pajamas, did we?

MC: No.

JC: No.

PC: So I get in my underwear, and I leap in this bed and the light's still on. And they said, "Last one in's got to turn out the lights." [*laughter*] And I have to go back. It was the worst thing. But it was so common in the family.

JC: This was also the time when Pat realized he was looking forward to going back to the Citadel. [*laughter*] He had it good at the Citadel.

AR: I think we're ready for some questions if anybody wants to approach?

AUDIENCE: I want to hear the story about your mother and the snakes.

JC: My mother, she loved snakes and she, I guess her grandmother—

MC: She married one. [*laughter*]

JC: She did. She always loved snakes, and her mother, our grandmother Stanny, loved snakes as well. So kids, we always would go to parks or whatever, and my mother would search for snakes, and we'd go with her and look for 'em. My father was scared to death of snakes, so maybe that's why my mother loved them so much. But we were always looking for snakes, and to this day if there's one in the yard, I'll go move it for a neighbor or something like that, and we would never kill a snake, and we always were around them. But like I said, my father was scared to death of snakes, so it was always fun.

AR: Anybody else have questions?

AUDIENCE: What did you do to make your aunt so upset in that restaurant in Chicago?

MC: She was a nun! [*laughter*] They are always mad.

JC: She was. She was bitter.

MC: She married Jesus. [*laughter and applause*]

KH: I think my Aunt Margie was really drunk, and just—it wouldn't have mattered what we did that day.

MC: Lord love her. [*laughter*]

JC: We also didn't know our relatives from Chicago very well. This is my father's family. We moved every year, and back in the fifties and early sixties, there wasn't a chance to fly and visit your relatives. And they never left Chicago, and we never wanted to go there. So we only saw them two or three times in my lifetime. So it wasn't often. We just didn't know them very well, and they didn't know us.

AR: Anybody else?

AUDIENCE: Do you know from your relatives if your father had been beaten, had been a victim of abuse as well?

JC: I think later on, one of my uncles who we became a little closer to, talked about a little more of the violence that they grew up in. So I think his family or his father was very similar, and they used to get hit quite a bit, and they didn't grow up under the greatest of circumstances. So I think later on we heard some stories about that. But they were also quiet about it and didn't wanna talk about it very much. And they weren't very happy to see Pat expose my father in *The Great Santini*. They weren't happy with that book at all.

AR: Yes, ma'am?

AUDIENCE: How did the rest of you feel when Pat wrote *The Great Santini*?

PC: Good question.

TC: Well, from my perspective, it was such a wonderful book. I thought he captured my father in the interactions with the kids very accurately in that book. And my father was very angry, but my reaction was I think very positive, and I just loved the book. And when I watched that movie, you know, there's imbedded in that, in one of the basketball scenes, images of my mother sitting behind Blythe Danner and my younger brother, Tommy, is one of the basketball players on the court. So I get to see them again, and so I love when I tuned into that movie.

JC: One of the comments I have about the book when it came out is, you know, we enjoyed the book. It was a great book, and it showed a lot of what happened in our family, but it was a novel, and it had different stories as well. What I don't think Pat did in that book is tell the truth about how tough my father was. And I think we grew up in a family that was a lot tougher than that, and people never believe us when we say that. My father was much meaner than that.

TC: Yeah.

JC: One of the quotes that we talk about is Robert Duvall portraying my father was like Bambi. [*laughter*] As my father was incredibly tough, and it was just a very difficult childhood, and I think Pat's captured that in more of his books after that. But, you know, people just don't believe us.

TC: In reality he would have aimed the jet to the house.

KH: When *The Great Santini* came out, and I read it, I loved the book but it was really difficult to have our story out there for me. It took me a long time to be able to deal with that well. You spend a lifetime of secrets, and it's hard for that change to come. But I love the father in that book, and I would have loved to have had the father in that book, but that's not who we had.

MC: One thing about that book, it had four siblings, and I always thought, how nice our family would have been [*laughter*] without the pressure of those last three, you know.

JC: Trust me, we would've been happy to not have been born into that family. [*laughter*]

AR: Yes, ma'am?

AUDIENCE: You've said in your interview with Walter Edgar that the humor in the Conroy family didn't come from your father, that he had no sense of humor.

KH: That was true.

MC: It was dry.

PC: When I grew up, and the kids may disagree—*the kids*—when I grew up, I did not know Dad had any sense of humor at all.

MC: Yeah.

PC: He never made me smile, never made me laugh. Never. He didn't do one thing I didn't hate. I hated when he walked into the room. I hated when he left the room. I just hated everything about him. When I sent *The Great Santini* up to my publisher, I had this beautiful woman, an eighty-two-year-old editor, and she wrote me back, and she said, "Pat, no father would ever treat a child like that." And I said, "Ann, I'm not even tellin' the whole story." She says, "It's not believable, so you have to soften it." So I ended up having to go into that book and have the Great Santini give the kid a flight jacket on his birthday. Dad never did anything like that. Send roses to his daughter on her first prom? Forget it. And I would ask them, did he ever do anything nice to us? Did he ever take us out for an ice cream?

MC: He taught me to drive. [*laughter*]

PC: What was that like?

MC: A screaming maniac. Carol and I were the students, and you would have a screaming maniac yelling in your ear as you're trying to drive down the road.

JC: And here would be one of his sayings, "That's exactly what I didn't want you to do." That's one of the things my father used to say.

PC: That phrase drove me crazy. The baby would spill milk, and the baby'd get hit. Okay? You know, bam! And then Dad would say, "That's exactly what I knew was gonna happen."

MC: "I knew that was going to happen."

PC: "I knew that was going to happen." And Carol and I were older. We'd say, "Well, why didn't you tell us, stupid?" [laughter]

MC: Goosh!

PC: Yeah, goosh! [gestures] But I was told it was not believable, so I had to back up with Santini 'cause I knew that this was 1976, and America wasn't quite ready. Now we're ready for anything. A father can chop up their child, microwave it, eat it as a Popsicle. But then we didn't know as much.

AR: Our question is "How did the community react after the book was published?"

PC: Y'all say how yours did.

KH: I'm happy to tell you my best friend at that time all that was happening is still in this room today. [applause] And her name is Nancy.

JC: When the book came out, they didn't know my father. This was in Beaufort so they didn't know it, and so they treated us well. But they were shocked by what they heard. But we assured them that it was much worse. [laughter] And they were also celebrating Pat's success. He was doing very well, and Beaufort loved him and has always supported him, as has all of South Carolina. [applause]

TC: It kinda gave you a little bit of cool to have a brother that has written a book and your friends talk about it. And so it kinda gave you a way to meet new people, and it's been a blessing. [applause]

AUDIENCE: Was there a moment when you forgave your father during his "great second act?" After your brother's death?

PC: This kid was tragic. For all of us it kills us. We can't talk about that time much. But Dad, in crying he said, "My baby boy, I lost my baby." And he said, "He always got the short end of the stick. Tom never had a chance." So when we were at the funeral, and I was sittin' beside Dad, and I put my arm around him, and—Do y'all remember?—he simply wept through the entire funeral. He didn't hear anything, didn't say anything, he just cried. Openly. Completely. And we got back, we had a little meeting, and I think we just said, "Okay, Dad has now shown he loves us. He can't say it.

He certainly didn't say it or prove it when we were children," But because of the way he acted about Tom, we figured out how he felt about us. And so we said, "Let's give it up. Let's let it go, and we can get through this as a family for the rest of our lives." And so that was a big deal for me. [*applause*]

AR: Thank you all so much for coming.

The Conroys Chat
in Charleston

Moderated by Catherine Seltzer, author of *Understanding Pat Conroy*, this conversation took place on November 15, 2014, in the novelist Anne Rivers Siddons's sun-filled guesthouse in Charleston's South of Broad district. Brothers Mike and Jim had come to Charleston to attend Pat's induction into the Citadel's Athletic Hall of Fame the evening before.

CATHERINE SELTZER: I want to begin by asking you about your early childhood. Pat begins documenting your lives in *The Great Santini* as his doppelgänger is a high school senior preparing to leave home. He hasn't talked a great deal about what life was like when you were young children, and I wanted to ask you a bit about that. Did you play with one another growing up? In a conversation I had with Kathy, she recounted a story about the older kids putting the babies in a wagon and pulling them along, sort of set free in the world. Is that what you remember as well?

JIM CONROY: Well, we were so involved with sports. I followed Mike. Mike always took us with him. He still does that now: he will include all of us. And Pat does the same thing. As young kids though, I followed Mike everywhere, playing sports. We played baseball, basketball, whatever. That was all the way through high school.

CS: And you all played basketball and baseball?

MIKE CONROY: We played some football too, but not organized football.

CS: Were you on the same teams often?

JC: Generally. Mike was on an older team. But he would play with his friends every day, and I was always there.

MC: I would bet that three hours of our day was spent playing basketball.

JC: Or some sport. We were outside. There weren't any video games or TV for that matter.

MC: After school or on Saturdays, you did your chores and you were *gone*.

JC: We were trying to get out of the house.

CS: Right. And did you have the same experience that Pat did of your dad not necessarily coaching you?

MC: Our dad was the most loving man. [*laughs*]

JC: A wonderful coach. He spent so much time helping us. [*more laughter*]

MC: He coached me in a third game basketball team, and that's the only time he ever coached me.

PAT CONROY: Did he teach you anything?

JC: Fear.

PC: I don't remember him teaching me one thing.

JC: I just remember him screaming at us.

MC: He may have given some suggestions about dribbling. Now he didn't shoot baskets like modern basketball players do.

JC: He was left-handed.

MC: He was left-handed, but all of us were right-handed. But he taught us how to bat left-handed because that's what he knew.

CS: So you were learning from coaches and other kids. Were most of your friends military brats?

MC: Yes. Every year we moved. You'd move to a new base, where you knew you weren't going to make friends until you started school. So you'd end up that summer not knowing anybody, and then you'd hit school. Then by midsemester, you've got some friends, and you make a best friend. And then by June, you're moving again.

Everybody on base did this. [*pauses*] I think they moved the pilots more.

JC: I'm convinced—and Kathy argues with me about this—that who-ever was over Dad wanted to move him just to get him out, because they hated him.

PC: Because he was an asshole?

JC: Right. So I'm convinced that's one of the reasons we moved more. Now Kathy argues with me vehemently and says, no, they moved him because he was smart.

MC: Well, you have to be pretty bright to make colonel.

JC: That's her argument too.

MC: Back then, if they needed the skills of a pilot, they reached out and moved him.

JC: Yeah, I'd go with [the argument that] they hated him.

MC: When we living around D.C., he moved to Intelligence.

JC: Now you tell me if that's not an oxymoron.

MC: No, he must have had something they were getting his opinion on.

JC: Dad was in Intelligence in the Marine Corps because there wasn't anyone in the Marine Corps who was intelligent.

MC [*to imagined audience*]: Hey, Jim is being facetious.

CS: Do you want me to make a note here that Jim doesn't speak for the family and we should send the marines after Jim? [*laughter*]

JC: Now, I have also recently discovered his report card from college. Remember when I sent that out? [Jim found one of Don Conroy's report cards among Pat's papers in the University of South Carolina Archives. Don had received Bs in economics and history, a B- in speech, and Cs in English, Latin, and philosophy. Jim forward for-warded an image of the report card to his siblings with the message "Confirmed. Dad was a dope."]

MC: Kathy and I looked at that report card, and there were Bs and Cs, maybe an A? . . . We thought, "What a great report card!" We wish we did that well!

CS: We were talking yesterday about favorite places you had lived, and you talked about the time you had spent in northern Virginia.

PC: Spring Valley Drive, wasn't it?

JC: That was beautiful.

PC: That was definitely the nicest place we lived. Of course you guys got to go to Hawaii. And I never saw that.

MC: But we shared that that attic room in Spring Valley. You know, my first room that I actually had that wasn't a basement, porch, or attic was in college. [*pauses*] Boy, there were some *rooms*. Jim and I and Kathy shared a room in Omaha, Nebraska, that was an unheated basement.

PC: There were a lot of one-bathroom houses.

CS: How did you navigate that?

MC: The only problem with a one-bathroom house with our family was on Sundays. After church, we would go back, and Dad would grab the Sunday newspaper and lumber into the bathroom. After about thirty minutes, we're outside saying, "Dad, we need to use the bathroom." [*As Don:*] "Be right out." Five minutes later: "Dad, we're dying. *We are dying!* Let us in!" [*As Don:*] "Be right out." Finally he would plop out, we'd rush in, and go, "Oh my God. What just died in here?!" [*laughter*]

JC: That was horrible.

PC: I slept in the Pensacola place. I slept in the Omaha place. *Nothing* was like Omaha. I even got rained on in Pensacola, but that was nothing compared to Omaha.

MC: It would get to be thirty below in Omaha. When Pat stayed there when he came home from college at Christmas, he kept saying, "My God, it's cold!" and we told him, "Watch this, Pat!" [*Mike makes a long exhaling noise to demonstrate that they could see their breath.*]

CS: So your parents, Tim, Tom, and Kathy were upstairs?

JC: No, Carol was living upstairs. She was a sophomore and junior then. She was a senior when we were in Orlando. [*Speaking sarcastically*] She had a joyous high school career.

PC: I think she really loved Omaha. She really loved that school.

MC: And then her senior year, we moved.

PC: That was a nightmare if you moved your senior year of high school. That happened to Kathy, and it happened to Carol.

JC: I always thought the first six of us went to three different high schools. Mike tells me he went to four.

PC: You're kidding, Mike—

MC: I count four, because when we moved from Orlando to McLean, Virginia—Falls Church—because I came from a southern school, they put me in algebra 1, part 1.

PC: Oh, you were in special ed! [*Jim laughs.*]

MC [*ignoring Pat*]: Because there was a fear we would be moving, I had to take part 2 in summer school. I had to go to Langley High School for that course. So it was Marshall High School, McLean High School, Langley High School, and then Pensacola.

JC: The point being, six of us in a row went to three different high schools, Mike being the exception. My youngest brother, Tom, went to one high school because we didn't move a lot at that point. But I think that's amazing. And the two girls were the ones who moved in their senior year. Isn't that sad?

PC: It killed Carol. I don't know what the result was for Kathy.

JC: I don't think it was as bad for Kathy because we went to Beaufort High. We were on double sessions because it was the first year of integration. She went to school from, I think it was 7:45–11:45 every day, which isn't that bad, and I went from 12:45–4:45.

CS: So you didn't really get to see one another then. Pat has written in several places about having to find your way each year. Did it feel overwhelming to start all over again every year?

MC: We thought everybody did it.

JC: It wasn't that bad. And there are benefits too. I would much rather have grown up in a town where I knew everybody and saw everybody through high school and could go back for my thirtieth anniversary, or whatever it is. But at the same time, going to college wasn't difficult because you're moving every year. When you compare it to somebody coming from a small town, all of a sudden they're at the University of South Carolina with twenty thousand students, and it's overwhelming for them. So I think there were benefits for us.

CS: You can be dropped into any situation and be fine.

MC: I think Pat bonded with his high school because he was the basketball star. He played all three sports. I bonded at my high school in Pensacola, but I don't think the others have the same experience.

JC: No, I certainly didn't. My high school was 90 percent Japanese.

CS: Oh right, in Hawaii.

MC [*teasingly*]: No wonder you didn't do well!

JC [*speaking to Mike with exaggerated indignation*]: I did perfectly well! But not as well as those kids. They were very bright. They worked very, very hard. I went to a high school called Aiea High School, which is the only high school in America with four vowels in its name. I would appreciate if you didn't laugh at this: we were the Aiea Aliis.

MC: What is an Alii?

JC: An Alii is a Hawaiian warrior. We struck fear into the hearts of other teams.

MC: In the spelling bee?

JC: We used to laugh about that name. Give us a few consonants. But, really, I liked the school. I thought it was a very good school.

MC: Why didn't you go to the University of Hawaii?

JC: Because Dad lived there.

MC: Big mistake. Dad was moving.

JC: A year later.

CS: So you came back to South Carolina to be *away* from family. Pat was the first to go to college when he went to the Citadel. Did that change the family dynamic?

JC: It gave us more room.

MC: Pat is seven years older than I am. When he was a senior, I was in fourth grade. When he left, it was kind of happy days: Mom was more nurturing. [*laughter begins*] Dad was calmer. [*laughter*] There was a lot of stress between my father and Pat. He was "The Great

Santini" when Pat lived there. He was "The Okay Santini" after Pat left. I'm joking of course.

JC: Pat and Carol kind of formed a triangle with Tom. There were a lot of mental issues with all of the three. [*laughter*]

PC [*objecting*]: The lowest of the low! Scumbag of scumbags!

MC: The happiest times we had were when Dad was at war. Would you all agree with that?

JC: Absolutely.

PC: I used to pray for war.

JC: We all used to pray for war.

MC: He went to Vietnam twice. Those were great years.

JC: They *were* great years.

CS: But when Pat left, it didn't change things necessarily?

JC: No.

PC: Here's what it changed for me: when I came back to Omaha—this was my first trip back, I was a freshman at the Citadel—I had no place to sleep. I had no dresser drawers. I had no closets.

JC: You had no place to sleep for one week of the year! We had to live with them the entire year. You were in a much better situation.

PC: I didn't understand that in our family, when you went to college, you disappeared off the face of the earth.

JC: In the summertime he went to basketball camp, and in college—let's point this out [*speaking to Pat*]: you know this, and Mike knows this, but Catherine might not—he had food. When we went to college, we did not. Mike, once again, saved me many times by providing food for me.

PC: Shoplifting.

MC: I also wrote a letter to Dad and Mom, thanking them for introducing me to poverty. I never knew poverty before.

PC: You used a great phrase—

MC: "The institution of poverty."

PC:—thanking them for introducing you to the institution of poverty.

CS: Did they respond to that?

JC: No. Nothing changed, but I felt better. But I think they may have done better with the younger kids.

PC: Dad did better. I don't think Dad knew until you wrote that letter.

JC: Dad came up and saw me in my senior year of college. It was February or March, and he gave me a check for something like $150. He had never given me anything through college. He always said that he gave it to Mom, and she was supposed to give it to us. But I had never had a check that big in my life, and that was so much money to me. I was just shocked. I think they helped Tim and Tom much more. Tim was on a meal plan.

PC: I went with Mike one time to what we called the mess hall—

MC: —the cafeteria. It was like *Animal House*.

PC: He was trying to show me. He told me, "Mom doesn't send enough money for food." So he's standing there while people are throwing stuff away. Mike is standing there, and as people would walk by, he would say, "Oh, you don't want that biscuit?" "Oh, you're not going to eat that apple?" And he would take it.

MC: My friends were feeding me my last two years of college. They were always really good to me.

JC: After my first semester, I got a job at the library. That saved me— getting two dollars an hour, twenty hours each week. So I would have $40 a week.

PC: How much was the meal ticket?

MC: $43.50.

PC: And Mom would send you—

MC: Mom would send me $40. That was for *everything* though.

JC: For Kathy and me, Mom said she was going to send us $25 a week. And Mom would send us the first check. We'd get it. The next Friday, Kathy and I would be waiting at the university post office for mail to be delivered, because we would have called her on Monday, saying, "Mom, are you going to send that check?" She's say, "Yes, I'm sending it today. You'll get it by Thursday." Friday would come—no check. Saturday would come—no check. We didn't have any money to eat. Sunday there was no mail. On Monday we'd call

Mom, and she would say, "Well, I mailed it last Monday." The next Monday would come, and there would be no check. We would finally get the check Thursday or Friday. Meanwhile I would have gone and written a check for $25. Of course it was going to bounce. There was no question. But we kept waiting for that check, and it came the next Friday. And it would have a post date on it that she mailed it that Tuesday, over a week late. So she was stretching out her $25 a week to $25 every two weeks. And that was after calling her and hounding her. We would be so mad. But literally, Kathy and I would sit outside the post office for two hours until they had delivered all the mail. And we'd ask, "Have you delivered it all?" And they would say, "Yes, it's all been delivered."

CS: Wow. [*pause*] I'd like to ask you a question not about money, but about coming to terms with the larger family dynamic. In the interview you all did with Walter Edgar, Kathy said something that really struck me. She said that *The Great Santini* was very difficult to read because she had lived a life of secrets. After creating a story for the outside world for so long, it would be jarring and maybe a little scary to confront the realities of your growing up. It made a lot of sense to me—

MC: I'm an open book. Growing up, I really thought everyone grew up that way. Back then, parents were strict. Maybe not as strict as Dad was—he wasn't strict; he was explosive. It didn't matter what you did; it mattered what mood he was in at the time you were breathing. I remember one time Jim and Tim were wrestling on the floor—we wrestled and fought all the time, but it was play—and I was reading a book. Dad comes home from work, gets pissed off because they are playing, goes over and hits them—*Goosh!* I'm reading a book, and I'm thinking, "How can I get in trouble?" *Goosh!* [*Pat and Jim laugh.*] It was because I was in the room.

Growing up you also had a hiding place when you knew Dad was in a bad mood. He would go room to room taking out his bad mood, but if you were in your hiding place, he wouldn't find you.

PC: What was the best house for hiding?

JC: Spring Valley Drive [the Virginia house].

CS: That's funny because that was your favorite house, too.

PC: It had an attic. In that house I remember knowing that if I could get the kids to those stairs, they were safe.

JC: I remember one time when I was in my hiding place in the closet, over on the side. Dad is going through and opens the closet. I looked up and went, "Oh [*pantomimes surprise*]. How you doing, Dad? I was just looking for some clothes." [*laughter*] *Goosh!*

MC: I think when I was reading *The Great Santini,* I kept looking for a little more substance. I kept looking for the fifth child to be discussed. [Mike is of course the fifth Conroy sibling.] I couldn't understand why he would stop at Kathy. I thought that fifth child would pop up somewhere. [*laughter*] And I thought he could have expanded that history a bit more. He could have "The Children of Santini," "The Grandmother of Santini," "The Father of Santini," instead of just jumping to *The Death of Santini.* I thought he had five more books there that he missed out on.

CS: I have a serious question along these lines too. You both have been very steadfast in your defense of the book, and so I am not asking about that. But if you had been writing your family history yourselves, would there be something you would include?

JC: The book is a novel. The book is not true. My father did not die at the end. All of us would say our father was much worse than the book ever could have been. The book made him into a nice man; he died as a hero. My father was really tough on people in general. He had a horrible temper. All of us have always said that if Pat had written the truth, it would have been a lot more shocking.

MC: What I think is interesting is that sure the Great Santini is Dad, but the central figure in our family was our mother. She was the strongest one. She controlled everything in that family. The movie doesn't really show that. Mom was the heart of the family.

JC: When the movie came out, the famous line that Dad said to you [Pat] is, "You and I got nominated for an Academy Award. Mom got nothing."

PC: Did you go to the opening? What I heard—I was not there, and Dad was not there—but when Duvall was beating up his whole family—

MC: That was when we were seeing the movie in Atlanta. We were in the middle row. Dad was behind me. I was sitting with Barbara. Duvall was bouncing the basketball off of the kid's head. The whole movie theater is filled with friends of Dad and Pat. It's a real tense scene. Everybody is silent; everybody is watching this horrible scene with the dad bouncing the ball off the kid. The kid is walking into the house. The dad is saying, "Come on, you wussy," or whatever. This goes on and on—I forget exactly what the words were. There was kind of a lull there and I said, fairly loud, "I'm glad I didn't beat that asshole in anything." And everybody died laughing.

PC: There was another time that during the scene when he was beating the family up, you leaned out and said, "Bambi." [*laughter*] Duvall was like Bambi compared to Dad.

MC: Dad always took credit for Duvall's career.

JC: He did. That was the first movie where [Duvall] was the leading man.

CS: Let me follow up on something. Mike, you said that your mom was really the heart of the family. One of the things that Pat has talked about in *The Death of Santini* and elsewhere is that you all have given him a fairly hard time about his depiction of your mother, which I gather isn't entirely consistent with the way the rest of you see your mother. The suggestion is that perhaps he has romanticized her in some way.

JC: When we were young kids, that was definitely how we saw her. As adults, our views changed. I don't know why.

MC [*laughing*]: It was when the checks didn't come.

JC: I think Mom had more problems than we realized. When we were young we thought she was a saint, and as Mike said—and I forget this—she was just the strength of the family. She was the person we were always around, and Dad was overseas. We didn't want to see our father anyway.

MC: She went through a divorce. They [the Conroy siblings] were in college. At that time military wives, if they divorced their husbands, they couldn't get military pay. So they got nothing. Dad paid child support, but she couldn't get any alimony. She couldn't get retirement. She didn't have any money except for child support. And she never worked. She didn't have much money to send anybody.

JC: She also changed too, at some point in her life. Her flaws were more apparent as we became adults. I wasn't as close to her. I don't know if Kathy and Mike felt that. Apparently not Mike. I'll let Tim speak for himself. We grew apart a lot.

PC: Tim was as tough as anybody on Mom. There's only one who adores her. [*laughter*]

JC: I think Mike adored everybody. He's kind of like that too.

MC: I even liked Pat.

CS: How did you feel about the divorce when it happened?

MC: We prayed for divorce growing up. We actually prayed for more wars and wanted to take him out.

CS: Were you surprised by it though? That your mom ended up filing for divorce?

JC: Yes, I was surprised that she finally did the right thing. Certainly the good thing.

MC: What it basically was about was that Dad wanted to live in a big city, and she wanted to live in a small town. And he said, "I'm not going to a small town." That's when she decided to cut the ties.

CS: So she was setting up house in Beaufort and imagining a life for herself that year that they were apart?

MC: She bought Pat's house. Pat's house was a beautiful house on the Point. He basically gave it to her for thirty-five thousand dollars. That house was on the market about five years ago for a million and a half.

CS: Let me ask about your parents' divorce again. Did it change your relationship with your parents?

JC: I don't think so. My father—we still hated him. Giving him the credit he deserves, he made a great change in his life. Maybe it was just because we were adults, and we could make decisions about not seeing him again—because we didn't see him often. But to change your life, to change your personality, to become likable, and to love your kids—he changed a lot, so I give him all the credit in the world.

CS: I wanted to ask you about that change too because it seems like there is so much that is positive about it—he became a better grandfather and a better uncle. Was there something painful about that too because you got to see a side of him that was denied to you when you were a kid? He would go to nephews' baseball games and basketball games, for example, when he hadn't attended to yours. There's something really hard about that, I imagine.

JC: I certainly brought it up enough to him, that, hey, he wasn't like that when we were kids. And our cousins didn't believe it. They still don't believe that he was a jerk to us growing up.

PC: Jim always has a very good point. Our cousin Ed played basketball at the Citadel. When I played basketball at the Citadel, Dad saw one game.

MC: Where was that game? It was in Virginia. Was it William and Mary?

PC: It was William and Mary. All you kids came down.

JC: I think that was the only game we saw in his career. In [Dad's] defense, living in Omaha made it kind of tough to get to Charleston. We went to the one game, and then we moved to Pensacola, and the drive to Charleston was a long one.

PC: And then I was out of school. But here's something the dark one [Jim] has pointed out to me—when Cousin Ed was playing, Ed thinks Dad went to forty-five games.

CS: That would make me envious, I think.

PC: It did Mike.

MC: I think he liked our cousins much better than he liked us.

JC: I think that was part of his change. He was retired, and he had time to go to the games. Our cousins tell us he went to every soccer practice they ever had in the summer. That he would drive them places—this was in Iowa. Here's another statistic that has bothered me a little bit—

PC [*laughing*]: Oh no! "Bothered me *a little bit?*"

MC: This has been weighing on his soul!

JC: I think I've brought it up in the past. Of our graduations from high school or college, how many did Dad go to for all of the kids? Did he go to your graduation from college?

MC: *I* didn't go to my graduation.

JC: No you didn't. Because it wasn't a big thing in our lives, because our father and mother weren't going to come. Who did we have there? We were going for ourselves. I think he might have gone to Kathy's graduation from nursing school. I don't think he went to Tom's graduation from high school, but Mom may have gone. [*Speaking to Mike*]: Did they go to your graduation at Pensacola Catholic?

MC: I don't think so.

JC: I think you came home that night and the next morning we drove—. [*Speaking to Pat*]: Did he go to yours?

PC: Here's what he did. I think y'all went to mine. Dad was there but he didn't go inside the building. He just stood outside.

JC: Having kids, I can't imagine missing a ballet recital, a sixth grade graduation, a high school graduation, or a college graduation. I can't imagine it. Yet he managed with seven kids never to go to anybody's. How do you do that as a parent? Not that it's bothered me. [*laughter*] Not that it's left a scar.

CS: And you told him at some point—

JC: He'd gone to every graduation of Uncle Ed's kids in Iowa. Every one of them. College graduations, eighth-grade graduations, all of them. Isn't that odd?

CS: It is.

MC: What I find so funny about Dad is that for a long time, if Dad woke up in the morning and wanted to go to, say, Iowa, he'd get in his car and go to Iowa, spend the day, and drive back to Atlanta. Now to drive—he needed a hip operation, so he couldn't move his foot from the gas to the brake. So in the last ten years of his life, to drive—in downtown Atlanta—he used his cane to push the gas and the brake. He always drove this old used car. He had plenty of money, but he'd drive a beater, just because he wanted to. Pat, for [Dad's] birthday, leased him a brand new car. We knew Dad was at the end of his days. He had colon cancer.

JC: Now all of us leased that car.

MC: We all took credit for it.

PC: We knew Dad was dying, and he always loved red cars. And so we got this car and told him, "Come outside; we've got something for you from all the kids." And it really surprised him. We had a very moving ceremony—

MC: —A lot of relatives [attended]. What was funny about this whole thing was when Pat got the car back after Dad died, he went and turned it in. In six months, on a car that was leased for twelve thousand miles, Dad had put forty thousand miles on it. And this is from a guy who is using his cane to drive.

JC: Also there's a guy who doesn't understand [the rules of] leasing a car for twelve thousand miles, who has his name on the lease. Pat had no clue.

MC: Dad would wake up and just decide, "I'm going to go to Orlando and visit John."

PC: He did. Dad put forty thousand miles on that car. The other funny thing is that the night we gave Dad the car we called Jim, because Jim wasn't there, and Dad wanted to talk to him. Later, I could hear Jim talking on the phone to Tim, and Tim's apologizing to Jim. He was saying that he and his wife, Terrye, had given all they could. They could only give five thousand, and how much did you give?

JC: I knew immediately that he hadn't given a dime. I recognize that my brother Tim is the cheapest human being. He's in the same class as my mother.

PC: Where did you all kill him on this one time?

PC: The funeral of Dr. John Egan. Everyone brought liquor and food.

JC: Lenore asked us to bring food for the dinner that night. Everyone brought hams, smoked turkeys.

PC: And what was it that Tim brought?

JC: A little summer sausage. We got him on that. [*Sarcastically*]: "Thanks so much for contributing this thing." Poor Tim.

MC: When Pat dies, I guarantee Carol will come down.

JC: Carol will give the eulogy. [*Pat laughs.*]

MC: She'll be dancing on the grave.

JC: Pat wrote about Carol quite a bit in *The Death of Santini*. By the way, we feel—at least I do, and I know Kathy does and Tim does—that he was overly generous to Carol. I think he's a little more worried about it, but really, he was overly generous. I fully believe that. He could have written a lot of the truth and nailed her. He made her a very interesting character, and I don't think she is particularly that interesting of a character. And I think she's brought it all on herself.

PC: Is that true? You just don't find her very interesting?

JC: She's an interesting character, but she stayed away from our lives and has brought it all on herself. I think the way you write about her, she comes out a lot nicer than any of us would have written about her. And so did Dad in *Santini*.

CS: Do you feel the same way, Mike?

MC: No, I worked in the field of mental health for thirty-five years. And Jim worked at the state hospital also. I've been telling these guys for years that Carol gets disability because of her mental illness. She is borderline. She probably has some affective disorder. She has a lot of problems. So I give a person a lot of leeway. Nobody wants to be mentally ill. [*Cassandra King, Pat's wife, enters the room. Mike says, for her benefit*]: Really, Sandra has been the root of most of our problems. [*laughter*] Write a book about her! Lay it on the line!

JC: I thought Sandra *was* Carol in the book. She acts just like her. I consider her to be just like my sister Carol.

CASSANDRA KING [*laughing*]: You're just saying that to make me feel better.

MC: It's transference. When Pat says Carol he means Sandra.

CS: Have you talked about the book with Carol, Jim?

JC: She calls me sometimes, but we kind of stay away from that subject.

MC: She doesn't call him. He's joking. Everybody tries to call her, but we get the answering machine. We don't get a call back.

JC: She does usually call on my birthday. Does she call on your birthday?

MC: She's funny. She will always call when I can't possibly be there.

JC: In twenty years, she hasn't missed sending me a birthday gift. It's usually early. It'll include my son Michael's gift with it. It's very nice of her, and she never forgets. This year, I haven't gotten it yet. Usually it's a week early.

PC: I got a card from her this year.

MC: It was a beautiful sentiment. It said, "From the one who's known you the longest."

PC: She loves Christmas and birthdays.

JC: She always remembers Rachel and Michael [Jim's children].

CS: I think it was Janice [Jim's wife] who told me at one point that Carol has been good to all of your kids. She stayed with your kids for a week at one time, is that right?

JC: We went somewhere on some trip, and I invited her down to Texas, and I paid her for babysitting. And also we weren't going to be there, and I think that's kind of her issue: she doesn't want to be with us. She flew in, stayed with the kids, made six hundred to seven hundred dollars, then we flew her back. She was very happy with it.

CS: So your kids have a really different impression of her than you do?

JC: Absolutely. They like Carol very much. It'd be nicer if she would reach out to us.

CS: Let me ask you too about the thinking you have done about your family in the last couple of months as you've been donating items to the new Pat Conroy Archives at the University of South Carolina Libraries. I think you have also gone through materials that are there. Has looking at that memorabilia made you think about your family in new ways? Maybe understand something differently?

MC: Everyone has donated except for me.

JC: I donated some stuff that Pat had written. Pat had given me a hand-written chapter of one of his books. When he gave it to me—

MC: When it didn't sell on eBay, Jim decided to donate it. [*laughter*]

JC: Pat had given it to me—and he has given me a few things—and he has said when Rachel gets to college or when Michael gets to college, sell this. You might get some money to help them get through college. So I kept it through the years. But I can't sell anything Pat has given to me. How am I going to do that? When I saw the opportunity to give it to the library, I thought, "It belongs there." It turns out that they didn't have that chapter in the collection. Pat has given me a couple of things, and I thought what better place to give those things than the University of South Carolina? Tim has done the same thing, as has Kathy.

MC: Let us just say one thing if we are talking about giving. Pat is very famous, but he could not be more generous to his brothers and sisters. He has always given his time—anything we've asked him, he'll drop everything to make it happen. If we come to his home, he doesn't worry if we're intruding. He makes time.

JC: He's always made his house open to us at any time. The house at Fripp Island, he has always given it to us freely. In addition to that, he's been more of a father figure than my father ever was. He's been great about being around. He has been very generous. As has my brother Mike.

PC: And now I understand my father's problem with these guys. [*laughter*]

MC: Dad wasn't enough of a disciplinarian, was he?

JC [*ignoring Pat and Mike*]: Pat was gone when I was young: I was going into the third grade when he left for the Citadel. So we didn't see him; we didn't grow up with him. But Pat has made an effort to reconnect with us as we got older. He always invited us for Thanksgiving or Christmas or whatever, and to be around his kids. I've loved being an uncle to his kids; they've been wonderful.

CS: Let me ask you one last question. In *The Death of Santini*, Pat writes a lot about the blurring of lines between fiction and experience, and about the impact that his books have had on your family. I've been thinking about this since I saw the interview you all did with Aïda Rogers at the South Carolina Book Festival. It was a packed room, and the audience was enthusiastic to say the least. Do you ever feel uncomfortable because of this? And I recognize the irony of an interviewer asking this, but you don't get to make decisions about your privacy in some ways. We know more about you—or we think we do—than—

JC: It's not like there's a lot that we could do about it. We live in South Carolina.

MC: In Columbia it is so rare for somebody to put together the name Conroy in relation to Pat Conroy.

JC: I've gotten it a lot. At the airport, the guards will ask. "Conroy? Are you any relation to the writer?" You pretty much get used to it. Having said that too, in going back to Pat's generosity—he's always included us in movie openings and other events, which he didn't have to.

PC: And I regretted it bitterly.

CS: Of course. I was waiting for that! Well, thank you very much for lettering me invade your privacy further. It has been great fun to be here today.

Actor Jon Voight and Peggy Conroy during the filming of *Conrack*, St. Simons Island, Georgia, 1972–1973

Peggy Conroy at the premiere of *Conrack*, adapted from Pat's book *The Water Is Wide*

Peggy Conroy with Georgia governor Jimmy Carter at the Atlanta premiere of *Conrack* at the Fox Theater. The photograph was later inscribed "To Peggy Conroy, It was a pleasure to meet you and to watch Pat's great story, *Conrack*. Jimmy Carter." Photograph courtesy of Kathy Harvey.

Col. Bruce B. Rutherford and actor Robert Duvall in Rutherford's office during the filming of *The Great Santini,* U.S. Marine Corps Air Station, Beaufort, South Carolina, September 27, 1978. Photograph courtesy of the U.S. Marine Corps Air Station, Beaufort.

Jim, Kathy, and Mike Conroy with Peggy Conroy,
Fripp Island, South Carolina, circa 1981

Peggy Conroy's family homestead in Rome, Georgia,
photographed circa 1985

Peggy and Pat Conroy in Rome, Italy, circa 1982

Pat Conroy on book tour for *The Prince of Tides,* circa 1986

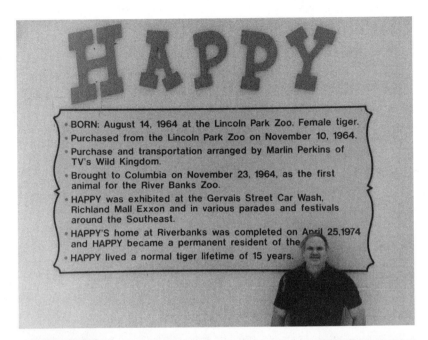

HAPPY

- BORN: August 14, 1964 at the Lincoln Park Zoo. Female tiger.
- Purchased from the Lincoln Park Zoo on November 10, 1964.
- Purchase and transportation arranged by Marlin Perkins of TV's Wild Kingdom.
- Brought to Columbia on November 23, 1964, as the first animal for the River Banks Zoo.
- HAPPY was exhibited at the Gervais Street Car Wash, Richland Mall Exxon and in various parades and festivals around the Southeast.
- HAPPY'S home at Riverbanks was completed on April 25,1974 and HAPPY became a permanent resident of the
- HAPPY lived a normal tiger lifetime of 15 years.

Photographs of Pat Conroy by the mural of Happy the Tiger at Riverbanks Zoo in Columbia, South Carolina, 1986, the year *The Prince of Tides* was published. Happy was the inspiration for the tiger in the novel.

Mike, Jim, Pat, and Tim Conroy at Barbara Streisand's party celebrating the release of the film version *The Prince of Tides,* New York, 1991

Pat Conroy and Cassandra King with dogs Tom and Virginia Woof, Fripp Island, 1998

Pat Conroy, Cassandra King, and Judge Alex Sanders at
Pat and Cassandra's wedding, Charleston, June 7, 1998

Pat and Don Conroy on November 13, 1997, approximately
six months prior to Don's death

Walter Edgar and Pat Conroy at the One Book, One Columbia keynote
conversation at the Township Auditorium, Columbia, February 27, 2014.
Photograph courtesy of Richland Library.

The audience looks on at the One Book, One Columbia keynote conversation between Walter Edgar and Pat Conroy. Photograph courtesy of Richland Library.

The Conroy Family Roundtable at the 2014 South Carolina Book Festival, Columbia, May 12, 2014: Pat Conroy, Mike Conroy, Kathy Harvey, Jim Conroy, moderator Aïda Rogers, and Tim Conroy. Photograph by Lauren Lyles.

Pat Conroy addressing the crowd at the Conroy Family Roundtable, 2014 South Carolina Book Festival. Photograph by Lauren Lyles.

The Rememberer

The following is excerpted from telephone interviews conducted in 2014 by author Katherine Clark with Pat Conroy for his oral biography, forthcoming from the University of South Carolina Press.

PAT CONROY: I've got blood pouring from every orifice of my body, but feel free to take a stab at me.

KATHERINE CLARK: I'll find a good vein. I always do.

PC: You may proceed, Dr. Bust-My-Balls Clark.

KC: I want to return to what you said yesterday about your family being in danger from the very beginning.

PC: Yes. We're all screwed up because we came through Mom and Dad. That was a difficult country to travel in, but we traveled it; we made it through; somehow we survived it. Tom did not survive. Tom can bring us to our knees. We all feel we failed him, left him behind, and were not watchful or vigilant enough to help him survive.

KC: How did the rest of you survive?

PC: Now the Bermuda Triangle [Kathy, Mike, and Jim], they always tickle me by saying they simply practice denial. Mike will tell you, "I love denial. It's the best thing." He says, "I worked for thirty-five years in the state mental hospital of South Carolina; none of my psychotics had any powers of denial at all. And I thought, a shame they're not like me. I have complete powers of denial. Something bothers me; I just deny it, deny that it happened." And Mike is perfectly happy with that definition of his life.

KC: A lot of people are.

PC: It would drive me crazy.

KC: Because you're a writer.

PC: I do not know if I was blessed or cursed with being the rememberer.

KC: Well, that's why you're also the writer.

PC: Yes. We writers forget nothing. Every one of those guys who went to the Citadel took it and left it behind. I left nothing behind. I remembered every instant, every guy that yelled at me, every guy that humiliated me. Just like I remember the utter horror which I grew up with. Kathy didn't remember a thing. The dark one [Jim] remembers some things. But it's odd: they don't remember much. They just don't. Carol didn't remember much.

KC: And Mike practices denial.

PC: Mike was telling me last night that I had once again shown him that he had chosen the right direction by going for pure denial. He had made the smartest choice he could. He said, "Pat, I know how you feel. You think I'm shallow and don't think deeply about things, and you're right, I got to admit that. But I'm not trying to leap off buildings. I'm not trying to take a thousand pills. I just deny it all happened, and I can get by just fine with it, thanks. I read all your stories and I think, yes, it's a shame it affected Pat that way. It ruined Carol's life. And old Mike, he just went to work, came back, had a few beers, watched a ball game, and that was it." And he says, "I think I by far made the best decision of anybody in our family." I said, "Mike, you got a point."

KC: But you've chosen the opposite path.

PC: I think the best country you can visit is that of the self, and if you've never done that, you've missed a great part of life. Self is an unknown territory to many people. It ain't to me. I dived into it. I tell every writer in the world: "Go deeper, go deeper, something is there." And then I say: "What are you hiding? What are you afraid of? What are you afraid to write? What do you not want to write?

What would you not write about under torture? Then you're getting close to what you should be writing about."

KC: Why do you think you're the one in the family who became the writer, the rememberer?

PC: Part of it is my mother read to Carol and me every day, and she did not have time to do that with the others. Seven kids, you know. And then I think my father did not go after the other kids the way he went after me. There was something about me as the oldest child, the first son, that he just couldn't handle. Maybe I came along too soon, interfered with his relationship with Mom. But when he beat me, there was a place I would disappear to inside myself. Marion O'Neill [psychiatrist] thought it probably helped me survive without becoming psychotic like Carol. It's the same place I go to now when I write. I guess I became used to going inside myself to survive what was happening to me.

KC: Have any of the others gone to a psychiatrist?

PC: My brothers and sisters, except for Carol, roar laughing at my shrinks. They have not done that. They should have, but they have not done that. And they say, "We don't need to, Pat. We read your books."

Translating Love

AFTERWORD

Nikky Finney

A boy grows up on a quilt of federal land, hopscotching geographies all of his life, until the twenty-third move, when he announces to his mother he will not move again. The boy has finally put his pen down into his ink and drawn his own lifeline into the soft South Carolina sand. He knows home is made of chaos, daily brutality, and his mother's writhing snakes. Figuratively he eats books to save himself. He has no idea where home is. But South Carolina takes him, pulls him in, and there in its rueful arms he stakes out the map of all the rest.

This writing boy will soon be the son of both the Citadel and Thomas Wolfe, where and in whom he will first find his tribe of passionate language lovers. He will always have a thing for falling in love with English teachers. He will meet the poet Archibald Rutledge at his South Carolina Hampton plantation and will be asked by the poet handing him afternoon tea, "Is it true you want to become a writer?" The writing boy will answer yes, and Rutledge will hand him a poem, one still in the making, and in that, Johnny-on-the-spot moment, the boy who eats books for a living will be asked to peruse its lines, and see himself into what is staring back at him and hopefully breaking through on the page. The boy will continue to find and eat words in his father's South Carolina house of melodrama, bruises, and violence, a house made of a fleet of swinging flying arms and inescapable eyes. His life will change forever because of the books. He learns quickly to "notice the details" and will from those moments forward, write with great and gorgeous attention, first and foremost, fiction or fact.

The boy becomes the great American writer who finds the courage to do what most do not have the courage to do. He writes about his father, even though it will mean the end to his relationship with his father's family, which has a history of belittling the children and belittling the mother, calling her loquacious southern equivalents to the iconic, but ever-black Aunt Jemima. No matter all of this. He can't and does not turn back. The line in the sand that he drew many years before is his line. He knows it. He keeps drawing it ever deeper, ever clearer. His father, the crazed, ballistic, slapping man, the marine, hands him the story of the Great Santini and it becomes the map of the young writer's southern life, its terrific highs and lows, and its slow death. On page after page there is familial pain beyond white flags, civil wars, beyond North and South.

In the midst of that great South Carolina place of reckoning, the southern funeral, the brutal father, screams out inconsolably into the air, unashamed and finally free. His son Tom has taken his own life, and the father cannot escape a father's pain and remorse. The funeral air hauntingly is filled with the sound of a man screaming for "his baby." This is the father of the boy raised on federal property—the boy who always wanted to be a writer, the son who was coaxed to always "notice the details," who is still growing into what he always desired to be, the gentle son, the wise brother, who finally, many years after this funeral scene, while in conversation with the tender circle of his adult siblings, reports back to them all, and finally to us, the listening in, that though the love of the father may have been hard to see, that does not mean we are not responsible for seeing it. He tells them— and us—something only he can tell, and when he does, all our eyes close slowly around his words. His words have everything to do with all our fathers, families, secrets, refusals, denials, "We have to translate how he loved us," the writing boy says,—"and we can do that."

Crazed, resilient, unhealed, driven, bloody South Carolina, a place difficult to describe, explain, is still a place that can be translated by those sons and daughters who do not disavow or cowardly change the details, who in the midst of unflinching, reflective, unrehearsed sibling conversation mine the riches of love at all cost.

The art of the conversation has the power to save each of us in this life, from each other's grand mistakes, and from our brutal personal and shared demons. The sanctified unabridged talk of brothers and sisters, hammering out who they are and how they came to be, has the power to start or end a war. The sound of such words holds the power to hang a man or cut him down. The music of such conversation reaches across to us there on the other side. All the shared writing and good talking sits the rest of us down with our own wounds in tow, other sons and daughters waiting, listening, leaning in, to what is being translated so that we might save our own lives too. In the listening we realize we too have the power, each of us, to turn ourselves into what we didn't know we knew about love so that we might urge our own intimates to reconsider the narrow dimensions of regret and tenderness lost.

Rich, loamy, sibling talk is complicated. The words and memories sear as they land and stick. I am grateful for the hearing of what I heard here. Grateful for what I know in my own life and for what I must make myself imagine and pull forward by way of this listening in. What is shared between those who have weathered the war, one voice over the another, giving each other space finally to tell the truth, to lie, to embellish, to get it right, to finish each other's thoughts or sentences, is enough to finally, gently, bury the guilty man, first hanged by the violence perpetuated upon him as a child, who became the general, who declared the war in the first place, upon the family, and among them, one by one, so that the great writer and his kin would one day hand over what matters to the rest of us. We modern day witnesses, of this very American, very South Carolina story, are now responsible for translating all of what we feel into all of what we know.

ABOUT THE EDITOR

WALTER EDGAR is the Neuffer Professor of Southern Studies Emeritus and Distinguished Professor Emeritus of History at the University of South Carolina. He is the author of *South Carolina: A History*, editor of *The South Carolina Encyclopedia*, and host of the radio program *Walter Edgar's Journal*.